CW01621362

Better Homes and Gardens®

HOME REPAIRS and MAINTENANCE

Better Homes and Gardens®

HOME REPAIRS *and* MAINTENANCE

Dennis M. Smith

All the information you need to confidently undertake home repairs

MURDOCH BOOKS
Sydney Australia

Pea-Beu
Nature
LOW ALLERGENIC
INSECT KILLER
WARNING
Brass
Scotch-Brite

CONTENTS

PART ONE

PART TWO

FOREWORD

If a home is to maintain its value, it requires some maintenance. The imperfections of their homes make most owners mutter things like, 'I wish I were a carpenter,' or 'If only I could change that!' The spiralling cost of building labour has created an economic pressure on people to do it themselves. Not only does that achieve a monetary saving but the psychological benefit from learning new skills is invaluable.

This book sets out to give you, the reader, a quick reference guide to enable you to do the typical jobs which you could well encounter in any one year. I have specifically written it to cater for Australian conditions and for people of both sexes who have had no prior experience in things practical. The book gives you all the information you need to allow you to confidently undertake and successfully complete small jobs.

If something goes wrong, simply blame me! Use some well-chosen swear words. I don't mind. Go back a couple of steps and make sure you've done everything correctly. The solution to all practical problems is in a methodical approach.

If you get too frustrated, leave the scene. Ring a friend or the hardware store and ask for advice. Finish a chapter of a blockbuster novel or compose a letter of complaint to the publisher of this book. Then come back and start again.

We'll do each job together, as a team. I know we can do it!

DENNIS SMITH

PART ONE

TOOLS AND MATERIALS

This part is included in the book because, if you are to become a successful do-it-yourselfer, you need to have a little knowledge about the materials and tools that you will be using.

I know, I know! You're already saying, 'Isn't a *little* knowledge dangerous?' In some instances, I suppose, that's true. I have therefore tried to include in this section all the *essential* facts, those which I judge to be necessary for your safety and success, given the space constraints of this book. If you want further information, besides standard textbooks on these subjects, many of the manufacturers or their associations supply, free of charge, printed information in the form of booklets and brochures on their products.

They also employ experienced technical staff to answer questions about particular problems. Use them! They love to show off their knowledge. They, like me, want to see you succeed.

Unless you're particularly eager to know about tools and materials at this juncture, I suggest you leave this section until you attempt your first job. Read the suggested procedure, then refer to this section and read about the respective tools and materials that are mentioned. That way you'll glean the necessary knowledge slowly, as you need it.

Basic Hand Tools

Doing minor maintenance jobs around your home requires some tools. This section describes some of the basic hand tools you should acquire with hints on their selection, maintenance and use. (The use of chisels, planes and saws, because of their complexity, is done in the relevant maintenance topics.) The sharpening of chisels and plane irons is included in this section.

Check with your closest *builder's* hardware shop to get advice on particular brands. I've stressed *builder's* because too often the person serving you in supermarket type stores knows little or nothing about practical things. Experience is a great teacher!

A nail punch is a useful tool for driving nails below the surface of timber before puttying and painting.

Hammer

A hammer is used for driving in nails and pulling them out. Be careful to select one that isn't too heavy. Try swinging it at an imaginary nail. If you can't control it buy a lighter one. Look for quality. Poor quality hammers eventually suffer from broken claws, chipped faces and snapped handles.

Clean the face with sandpaper occasionally to keep it from slipping off the nails and painting your fingernails blue! When extracting nails, put a scrap piece of timber under the hammer head so you don't mark the timber.

If you keep missing the nails, get a scrap piece of hardboard and bore a small hole in it (see picture on right). Start the nail, then put the hardboard over the nail. Then if you miss, you'll hit the hardboard, not the timber. If the timber is hard, rub candle wax on the nail to make driving easier. Or you can drill a hole, one slightly smaller than the nail thickness.

Use a hardboard nail foil to avoid damaging the timber you are working on.

Hammers

Nail Punch

A nail punch is a useful tool for driving nails below the surface before puttying and painting. Get two different sized ones (a fine and medium) to suit different gauge nails. Don't use a fine punch on a large nail or you'll ruin the end. Punches are also handy when used for making pilot holes to drive small screws into.

Pliers
Pliers work like your dentist's extraction pincers and can cut wire, grip nails, and, if you don't have spanners, provide a crude method of loosening nuts and bolts.

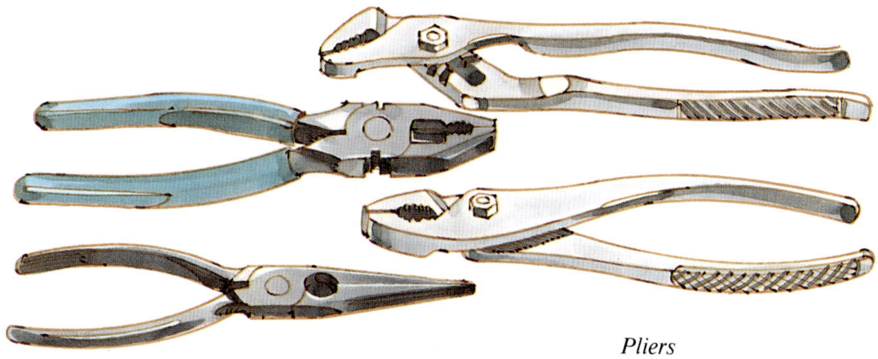

Pliers

Tape
A tape is an accurate, easily stored measuring device. Get one that extends to at least five metres so you can measure long lengths. Buy one with clear numbering and divisions and, whatever you do, don't bend it or it may crack. Try not to get it wet but if you do, carefully dry it before storing otherwise it will rust.

Pencil
A carpenter's pencil, with its thick lead, will not wear out as quickly as an ordinary lead pencil. You can get various grades of hardness. Pencil lines can be more easily cleaned off than pen. For accurate work pencils should always be sharp. A chisel point stays sharper longer.

Spirit Level
A spirit level is essential for accurate levelling (making things like bench tops, door heads, etc., exactly horizontal) and vertical truing of window and door stiles, etc. The longer it is the better. A 900 mm one is ideal.

Spanner
A spanner is used for loosening or tightening nuts. One that opens out to 25 mm will do most jobs.

Square
A square is a very useful tool for marking lines square to each other. Possibly the best one for the handyperson is a combination square. This useful tool can be used for making right angles, marking 45° lines (for mitring), and, with the blade slid back into the handle, for gauging pencil lines parallel to one edge.

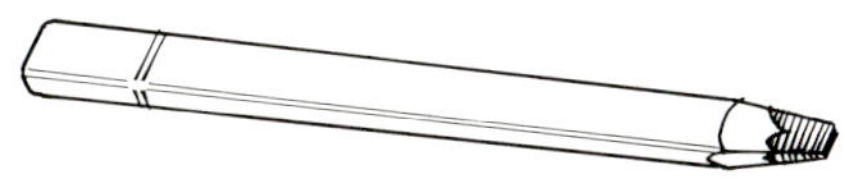

An adjustable spanner is an indispensable tool for loosening or tightening nuts.

Plane

A plane is used for reducing timber to size or making it smooth. There are many types and qualities. I'd recommend you get a jack or a smoothing plane. Again hold the plane before purchasing and pretend you're planing. If your arms feel as though they want to fall off, get a smaller one that you can control.

There are many brands on the market. Some of the cheaper ones may break, which means they are no longer cheap. It's a question of relating cost to potential use.

The parts of the plane are shown in the drawing below. When you've finished with it, wind the blade back in and store the plane in its box. A light rub of oil helps to prevent rust (for use see Planing Procedure in Sticking Doors).

A smoothing plane should be comfortable to hold. Check carefully before you buy.

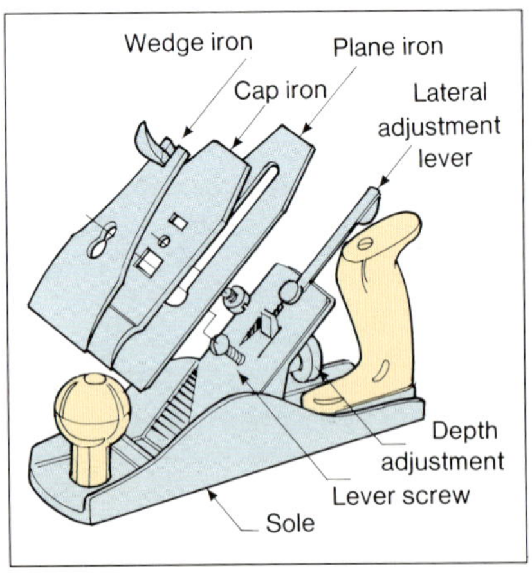

The parts of a plane

Check the adjustment of the blade of the plane.

Sharpening Planes and Chisels

You'll need your oilstone and some light machine oil mixed with turps or kerosene. The oil floats away the metal particles while the solvent cleans the stone.

To sharpen a plane iron (or chisel), first coat the stone with a layer of the lubricant. This layer, which should be re-applied throughout the sharpening operation, will keep the stone cutting.

1 First extract the plane iron. This involves taking off the lever cap iron (see drawing on this page) and removing the double iron. Undo the screw and swivel the backing iron at right angles, and then slide it down until the screw head comes out of the hole in the plane iron. Examine the plane iron carefully. If it's gapped or if the bevel is rounded, get the plane iron reground at a knife-sharpening outlet or hardware store.

2 Lay the plane iron (or chisel), bevel down on the stone and then lift it up until the oil squeezes out. This means the grinding angle is against the stone.

3 Lift the end of the tool a further 10 mm and, locking your wrists, begin to rub the plane iron along the full length of the stone. Use the whole width of the stone (see page 16).

4 Lift the plane iron up and feel the flat side for a burr. If there isn't one or it's only part way across, repeat the process. Once the burr is full length turn the plane iron over, lay it on the stone and, being careful not to lift it (or you'll make a bevel on the flat side making it impossible to sharpen), take off the burr.

5 Repeat the procedure several times, pressing more lightly and with fewer strokes each time. On the final one make only one stroke on each side. If you've followed the procedure correctly you should have a sharp tool. To check if it's sharp, run your finger *lightly* along the edge from the flat side. It should, if sharp, slightly nick your skin.

When putting the plane iron back in, be careful you don't let the sharp edge touch the backing iron (which must be set 1 mm back) or any other metal surface.

Planing a small block

File and Rasp

A long, flat file and a rasp with both a curved and a flat surface are useful for many jobs when it's hard to plane or saw.

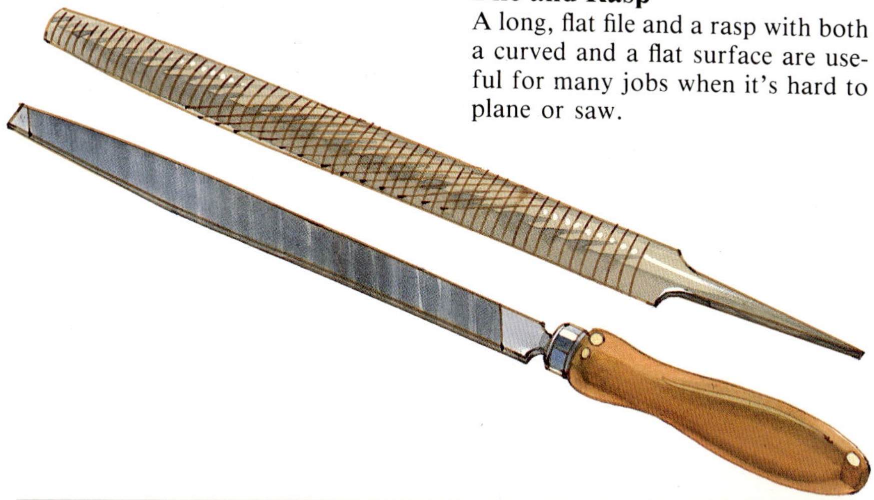

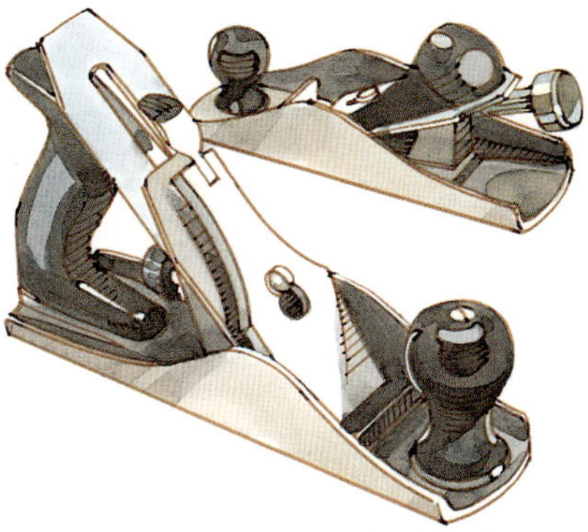

A block plane (above) and a bench plane (below).

Chisels

Chisels are used for chopping holes in, or paring away, timber. There are many types of chisels. Buy two for starters: say a 10 mm and a 25 mm firmer chisel with either a plastic or a steel-ferruled wooden handle. These chisels are good for general work and will stand up to rigorous hammering or levering.

When not in use, put your chisels in a cardboard box so the edges can't touch any metal or children. And remember NEVER put your hands in front of the blade while chopping or paring (for use see Filling a Hole in Timber).

A file can be used to finish off the edges of a variety of surfaces and materials.

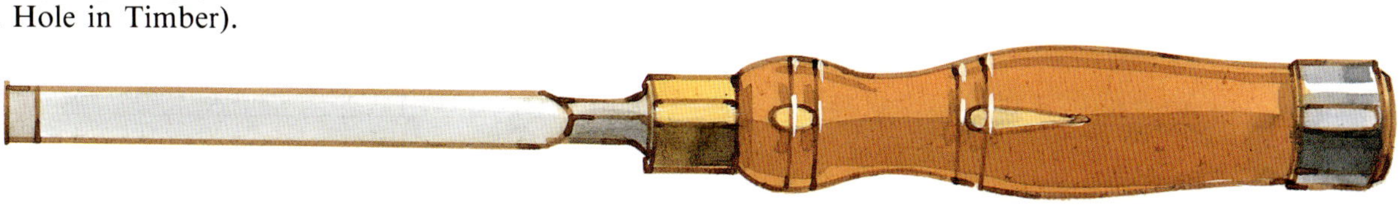

Chisels

Use a hacksaw for cutting metal and plastic. There are different blades available to suit various materials and kinds of metal.

A coping saw is used to make circular cuts. Drill a hole to start.

Saws

Saws are used for cutting things to length. For fine joinery work a tenon saw is useful. For more ambitious projects which involve larger timber sections you can add a panel or handsaw. The tenon saw, with its rigid back, has very small teeth. Don't be deceived — they cut wood or flesh with ease so keep your hands away from the cutting edge.

An inexpensive but handy saw is the coping saw. It is used for scribing or making circular cuts.

A hacksaw is used for cutting metal and plastic. There are many different blades available to suit various metals.

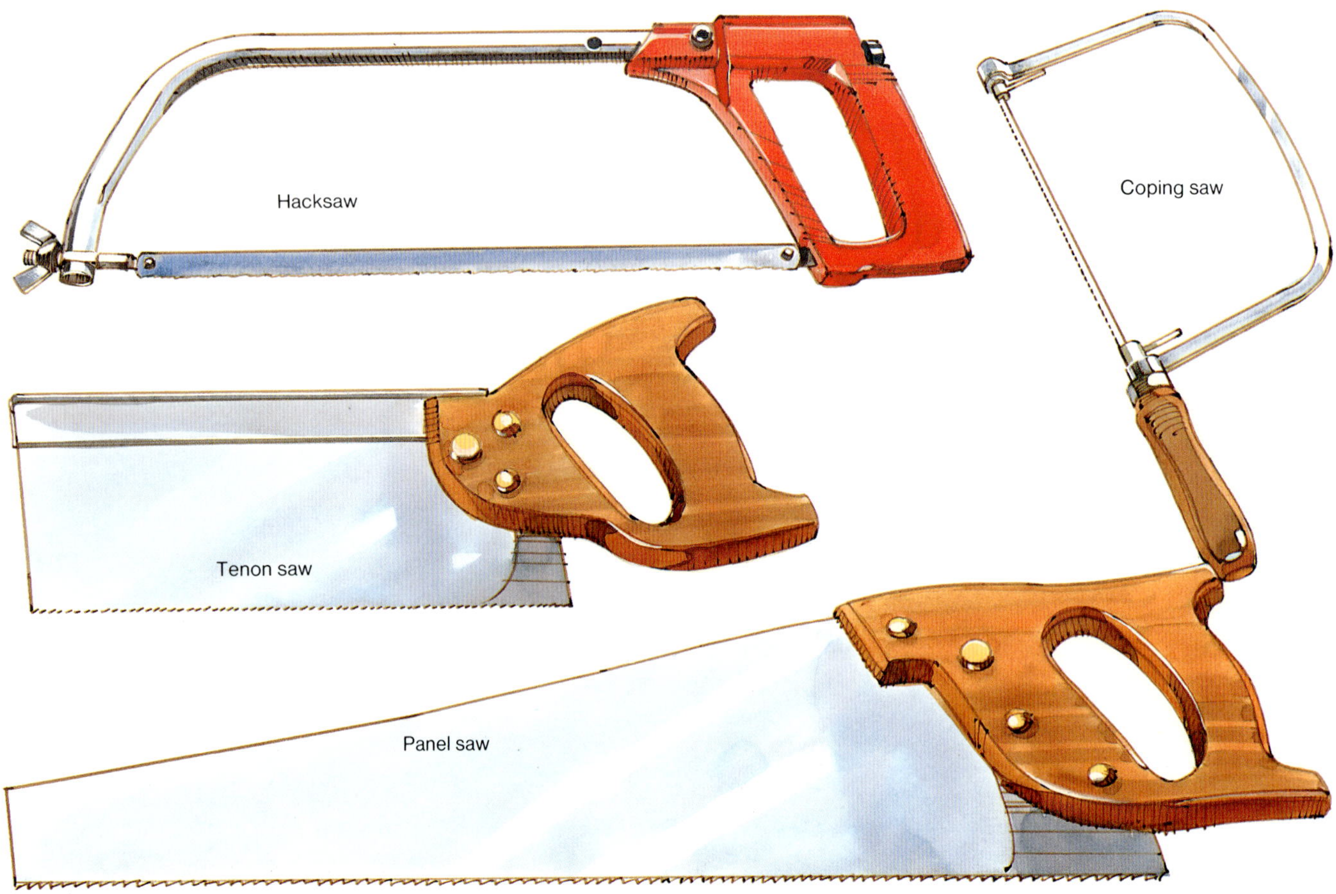

Hand Drill

A hand drill is a useful tool which, in combination with various drill bits, is handy for drilling holes for plugs or screws. It works on the same principle as your hand eggbeater.

The turning handle spins the chuck which holds the drill bit (a touch of oil on the drive wheel will lubricate the turning action). To put in a bit, hold the turning handle still and unwind the chuck until the bit slips into the jaws. Then simply tighten the chuck with one hand while immobilising the turning handle.

As an alternative to buying a hand drill, you can hire electric drills (see Electric Drills under Basic Electric Tools).

Drill Bits

Get a set of drill bits to suit home use. Your hardware store will advise you on quality but they should range between 2 mm and 10 mm. A 6 mm masonry bit is handy if you have brick walls.

A countersinker is used in a drill to produce a neat finish for screws.

A hand drill is cheap and is a very useful tool for tight situations or fine work where the electric drill is not needed.

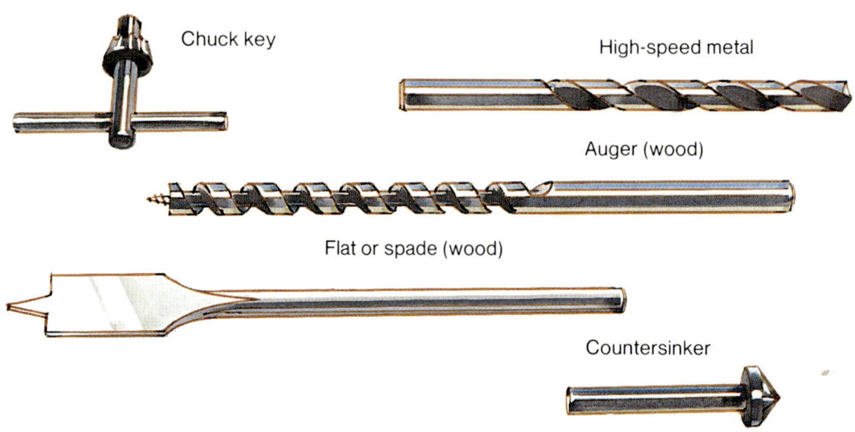

Screwdrivers

Screwdrivers are for driving in or removing screws. The tips of screwdrivers are shaped to suit various profiles and sizes of screw heads (slot head, Phillips head, etc.).

The important thing is to select the right-sized screwdriver to fit the screw. One wider than the screw head will damage the timber and one too small will ruin the slot of the screw, making it impossible to get it in or out. Keep in mind that a screwdriver with a large handle is easier to get both purchase and weight on than a small one. A ratchet screwdriver allows you to turn the screw without having to move your grip with each turn. It can be adjusted for driving or removing as well as being fixed.

Buy a small set of mixed screwdrivers to begin with and perhaps one with a ratchet. You can add special types as the need arises.

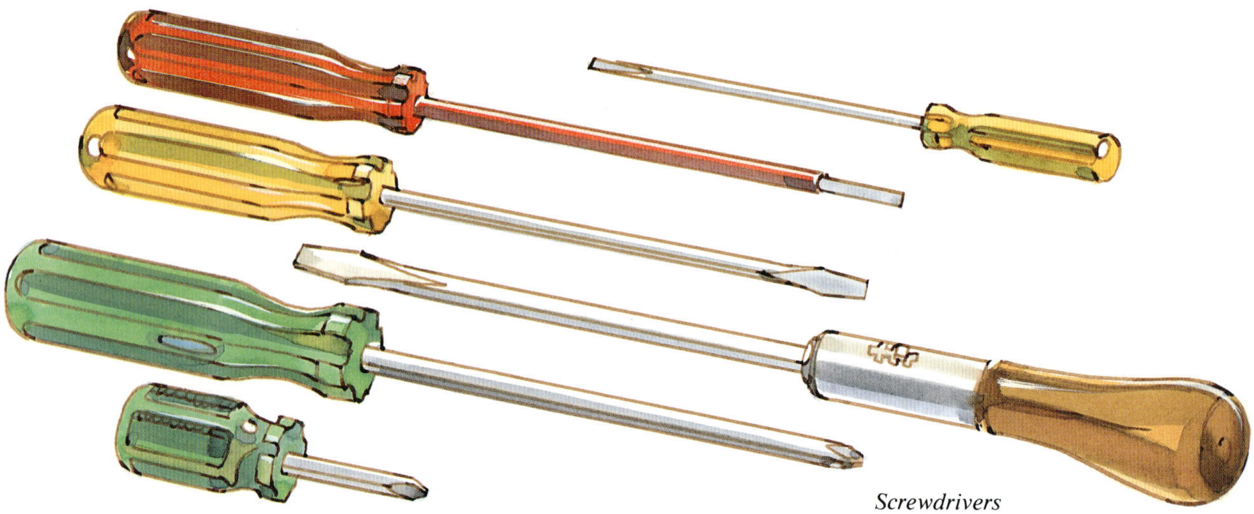

Screwdrivers

Use a well-oiled stone to keep tools like chisels and plane blades sharp and working efficiently.

Oilstone

Natural stones are the best but the most expensive. For the do-it-yourselfer, a synthetic stone is adequate. Your stone, kept in its box, should last for years. Left on a bench it will soon get chipped or cracked.

Trimming Knife

With its renewable and retractable blade, a trimming knife is handy for cutting plasterboard, vinyl tiles, plastic, etc.

G-Cramp

A couple of G-cramps are handy if you are doing some single-handed jobs or gluing. Always use two scraps of timber underneath the jaws to avoid damaging the timber of the job you are working on.

Obviously there are many more tools you can acquire but for most of the jobs described in this book, these ones will suffice.

A G-cramp is very useful if you are doing some single-handed jobs or gluing. Always use a scrap of timber under each jaw to avoid damaging your timber.

Basic Electric Tools

There are many electric tools available, many of which take the drudgery and hard work out of home maintenance. The three that are generally the most useful are the electric drill, the circular saw and the sander. As with hand tools, quality is important — that and adequate power (not too little, not too much). Before you select, keep in mind the old adage: you usually only get what you pay for!

When buying a tool, check whether it is designed for a tradesperson or a handyperson. A tool for the handyperson is too often poorly made, or underpowered, or both. Such a tool may soon burn out or spend much of its life at the repairers. Go to where the local builders buy their tools and ask for advice.

An electric drill is a boon, and a necessity if you have masonry walls.

Electric Drills

Although most drilling can be done with a hand drill, an electric drill is a boon. If you have a home that has masonry or rendered walls it is a must. A popular size is one with a 6 mm chuck. It will hold most standard drill bits and, if it's good quality, usually has sufficient power to cope with boring into the occasional hard brick. Of course, if you have the money, a drill with a 10 mm chuck, especially if it has a hammer facility, will give you years of effortless service.

The question of whether it's better to buy a cordless drill or one with the conventional 240 volts is a hot issue. I admit I'm suspicious of battery-powered electrics, but then having to run extension leads everywhere can be a nuisance and sometimes, in wet weather, dangerous. Cordless drills generally cost a bit more, have the same warranty, but have a limited use capacity (two to three hours) whereas you can drill all day with a standard one. But then there is no chance of electrocution and, if you only use it for small jobs, it is very convenient.

Prices range from eighty to seven hundred dollars plus. A 10 mm, conventionally powered 7.2 volt unit with a hammer action (they come in 4.8, 7.2 and 9.6 volt capacity) is the one I'd probably buy for myself but then old habits die hard.

To complement your drill, you'll need a set of drill bits (2–10 mm). A 6 mm and a 10 mm masonry bit are handy for drilling into brick or stone. A set of speed borers makes drilling large holes in timber a breeze.

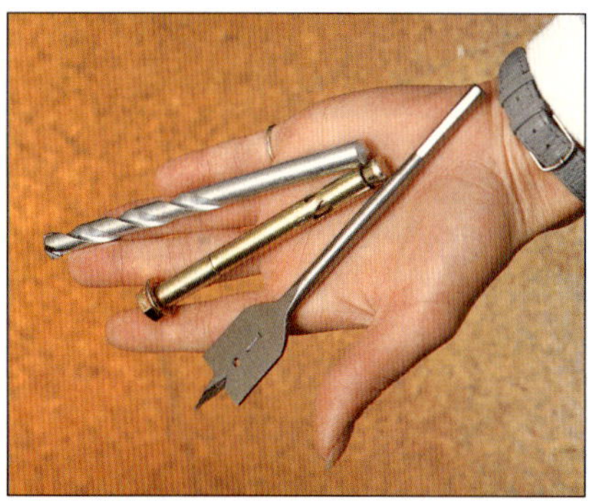

A masonry drill bit, a masonry bolt and a speed drill for timber.

An electric drill makes short work of boring a hole in masonry walls.

SAFETY POINTS WHEN DRILLING

- Turn off the power when putting in the bit.
- Make sure the drill is tight by using the chuck key.
- Properly secure the work to be drilled.
- Make sure no loose clothing or hair can get wrapped around the chuck (unless you want to be naked or bald).
- Turn on the drill and check the bit is in the centre.
- Make an indentation in the work (with a punch or nail) so the drill stays in the centre of the hole.
- When drilling deep holes, withdraw the drill several times to clear it.
- Don't stand in water while drilling or let the lead dangle into a puddle.
- Wear rubber-soled shoes for added safety.

Circular Saw

Few electric tools have the popularity of the circular saw. Yet it is possibly one of the most misused and therefore potentially dangerous tools on the market. Every year it severely lacerates or lops off numerous fingers and thumbs, to say nothing of fatalities.

Like the electric drill, its work can be done, albeit much more slowly and laboriously, using a hand tool such as a panel or tenon saw. Again the choice is one of considering the high cost against the ease, quickness, and of course, the likely amount of use.

Circular saws come in a variety of blade sizes with the 185 mm ($7^1/_4$ inches) being the most useful one for the average do-it-yourselfer. Of course, the larger the blade, the more robust and heavy the saw will be but keep in mind it will also be more difficult to control.

Again go for quality. It will be reflected in the solidity of the base frame, the design of depth and tilt adjustments, and, most importantly, the efficiency of the telescoping guard (which keeps the blade isolated from your precious fingers).

Although it's expensive, buy a tungsten-tipped blade for your saw. You'll rarely have to have it sharpened (unless you continually cut through nails) and the cut it makes looks as if it has been planed.

A circular saw is a most useful tool, but care is needed when using it.

SAFETY POINTS WHEN SAWING

The work should be held tightly with clamps or temporary nails so that you can keep *two hands on the saw and two feet on the ground* at all times.

- Unplug the saw if adjusting it.
- Set the saw depth to cut a fraction (say 3 mm) more than the timber thickness.
- Support the work in such a way that it won't close in on and jam the saw blade.
- Never stand behind the saw when cutting in case it throws back at you.
- Keep the work area clean so there is nothing to trip on.
- Make sure the lead is well clear of the blade at all times.
- Most importantly, never immobilise, hold back, or remove the telescoping guard (unless you would like to be permanently short-handed!). It's against the law for starters and incredibly dangerous.

Orbital Sander

Although more expensive belt sanders are available, they are probably too difficult for the beginning do-it-yourselfer to use successfully. The orbital sander has a place if you are predisposed towards electric tools and saving energy. However, for the best finish to timber, nothing really beats careful planing and a final rub with a cork block and abrasive paper.

An orbital sander gives a smooth finish with little effort. The model in the picture has a dust bag.

The orbital sander is primarily a finishing tool, one that is used after scraping and planing. It cuts very slowly so it won't flush off badly fitting joints or sand smooth sawn timber but then neither will it ruin the job. Go for a large capacity one otherwise the cutting action will be so minimal as to be useless.

It is a safe tool to use, so no particular safety aspects, other than the general ones that apply to all electric tools, need be considered. Use different grades of abrasive paper to achieve a good result (a coarse one to start with and a fine one to finish).

Hint. Alternately holding the sheet at diagonally opposite corners, run the smooth side of the abrasive paper sheet over the sharp edge of a table. This will make the backing sheet more flexible and less inclined to crack.

Timber

Timber is one of the most versatile yet easily worked materials available for home and furniture construction. It is relatively light, strong, flexible, and has a natural appearance which, when covered with a clear finish, gives a warmth and variety that few synthetic materials possess.

There are many species, each one of which has advantages and disadvantages. Timber comes in an amazing variety of sizes, profiles, and combinations (plywood for example). Timber also forms the basis for many manufactured building products such as particle board, hardboard, etc.

Popular Types and Uses

While the indigenous Australian species are mainly hardwoods, some exotic types are now grown commercially while many more are imported. The result is a bewildering array of choices for you, the do-it-yourselfer. Because space does not permit a full coverage of every species, I have included only the major ones that you should consider using.

Before you select a particular species, ask yourself the following questions.

- Is it to be used internally or is it partly or completely exposed to the weather (the sun being most destructive)?
- Is strength important?
- Is appearance important?
- Should it be termite and fungus resistant?

Answers to these four questions will narrow the range of choices considerably.

Western red cedar This attractive Canadian timber typically ranges from light straw or a pale reddish colour through to a deep brown. It has a high resistance to termites and fungi, stands up to the elements well, has limited strength and is, relatively speaking, inexpensive. (Californian redwood, which has similar characteristics, is much more expensive.)

Though soft and easily damaged, it is used extensively for windows, external doors and door frames, and outdoor furniture. It is also sawn into weatherboards for cladding, and milled into a variety of shiplap and lining boards for use in feature walls or as a lining for bathrooms. It takes paints, stains, oils or waxes with equal enthusiasm.

Oregon (Douglas fir) This pine, mainly imported from the USA and Canada, is widely used as a structural and joinery timber and is easily sawn, nailed and planed. Its lightness, strength, flexibility, attractive yellow colour, and relatively good weather resistance (if painted) are its strengths. On the down side, it has little termite resistance, has a tendency to have seeping gum pockets, splinters easily, and the ends will split badly if not sealed.

It comes in various grades depending, amongst other things, on the number and size of the knots. You should clearly outline what you want it for so your supplier will give you the correct grade. (The price goes up in quantum leaps with each improvement!)

Radiata pine This straw-coloured Californian timber which, grown locally, makes up 20% of all sawn timber, is widely used for framing, joinery, furniture, benchtops and panelling. Its cheapness and easy workability assist its popularity.

In its natural form it is not durable in exterior situations (Cypress pine is better), but when treated with a copper chrome arsenate solution under pressure, it becomes durable and is widely used for decks, wall cladding, lattice, etc. Sold as logs, the treated pine is used for playground structures, log cabins and pole houses.

Australian hardwoods Varying in colour from straw to pinkish brown to dark red, these heavy, hardwearing, close-grained timbers are used in many structural (posts, joists, bearers, wall and roof framing), joinery (flooring, window sills, etc.), and furniture applications.

For in-ground contact use dur-

Western red cedar

Oregon

Radiata pine

Australian hardwood

able species such as tallowwood or red gum (treated hardwoods are also available). These two can be used above ground together with blackbutt, turpentine, brushbox, etc. Well known decorative hardwoods include silver ash, coachwood, Tasmanian oak, red mahogany and karri.

Pacific maple

Many of these hardwoods, over time, achieve a rocklike hardness and have been known to bow somewhat dramatically. Many carpenters shudder when confronted with a hardwood frame because of the weight but once it's there, white ants permitting, it should last forever!

Pacific maple (Meranti) This popular, easily worked joinery timber, which comes from exotic places like Malaysia, Indonesia and the Philippines, is used extensively in Australian home construction for jambs, architraves, skirtings, shelving, doors and plywood. It is not considered suitable for external use.

Though its strength varies (usually the darker it is the stronger), it saws, planes and sands easily and, like cedar, readily takes most timber finishes. Because of its abundant supply it is fairly cheap.

Timber Profiles and Sections

If you go into a large timber yard you will find a bewildering array of timber sections (round, square and rectangular shapes) and profiles (irregular shapes). For general home maintenance you will only need to be acquainted with the ones described below.

These timbers are sold either

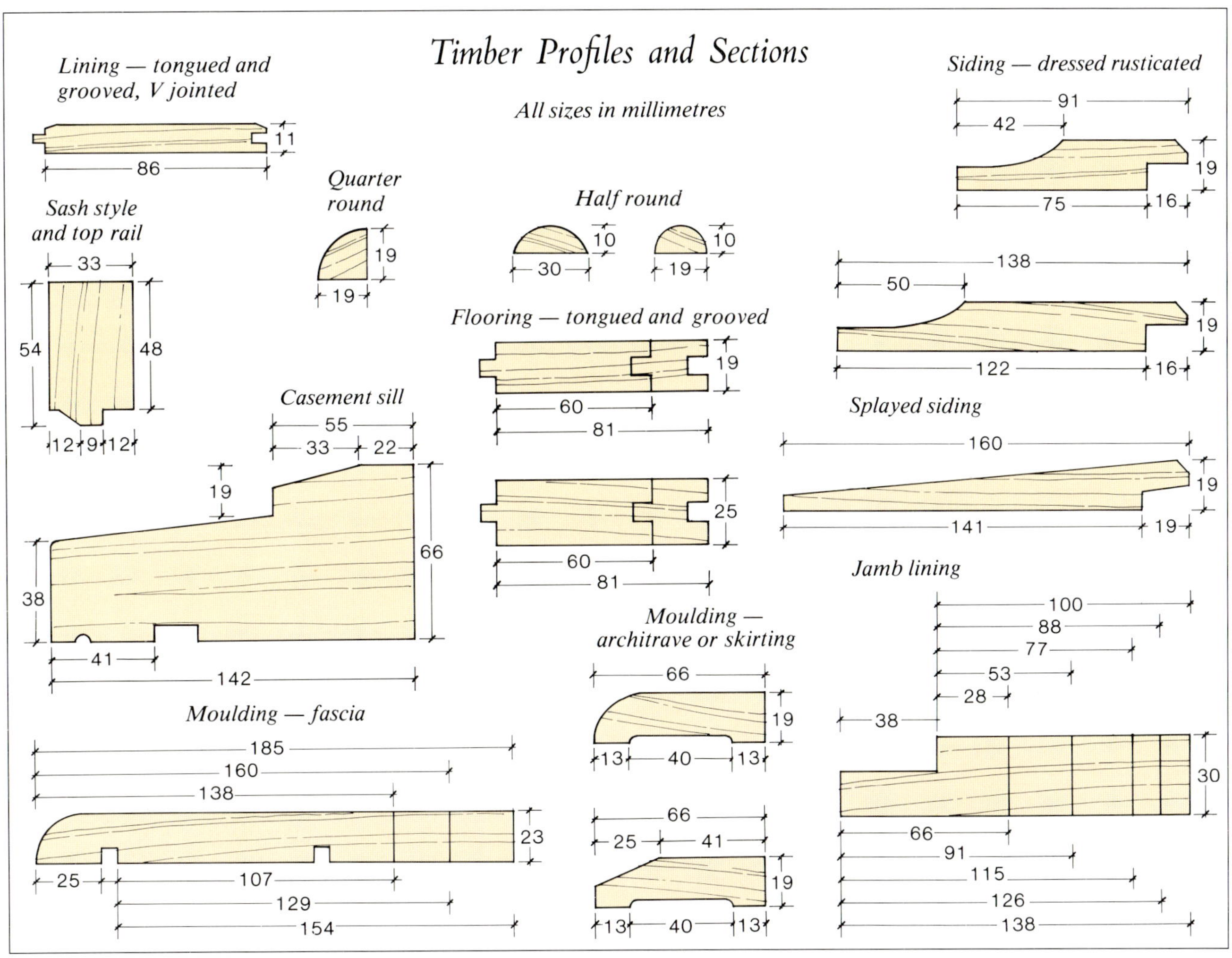

sawn, that is, straight off the saw (which gives a rough but even finish) or dressed (that is, fed through a thicknesser so the wood is smooth and usually only requires some sandpapering before applying a finish). Dressed timber is more expensive than sawn not only because of the extra work involved but also because dressed timber is usually better seasoned (has a lower moisture content to lessen the potential shrinkage).

Common sections

Battens range from 25 mm × 25 mm (1 × 1) through the popular 50 mm × 25 mm (2 × 1) up to 75 mm × 38 mm (3 × 1½). In a sawn state they are often used for roofing, and when dressed, for supporting shelves.

Scantlings typically range from 75 × 50 mm up to 300 × 75 mm and in a sawn form make up the bulk of structural timbers such as joists, bearers, plates, studs, noggings, ceiling joists, rafters, etc. When dressed they are used for posts, handrails, etc.

Common profiles

Jamb. The frame a door hangs in is made from jamb material. It has milled into its surface a single or double rebate (which can also be formed by nailing on a stop). Entry doors usually have heavier jamb sections than internal ones.

Architraves are trims that fit around doors and windows and provide an attractive finish.

Skirting hides the joint between the flooring and the internal walls. It is usually wider than the architrave and should have the same profile.

Quarter round (quad) is a useful mould, which ranges from 50 mm (2 inches) down to 13 mm (½ inch), finishes off a variety of right angle corners.

Flooring. The tongued and grooved joint hides shrinkage and seals out draughts and dampness. Widths range from 75 mm (3 inches) up to 150 mm (six inches). It comes in both hardwoods and softwoods.

Sill is found at the bottom of a window and is often made from tallowwood. This profile is milled to suit the type of window (box frame, casement, etc) and the type of wall frame (brick veneer, timber frame, etc). The slope helps to shed water while the small groove underneath it forms a drip which stops the water from running underneath.

Window head and stile. Rebated like a jamb, this profile is used for the side and top members of timber window frames (not box frames, which are made up from a number of different profiles).

Sash stock is used to make the frame that the glass fits in. It comes in a variety of sizes and mould shapes depending on the size of the window. Typically the lowest member (the bottom rail) is wider than the sides (the stiles) and the top rail.

Linings. Thinner than flooring but having the same tongued and grooved joints (unless it's shiplap), linings come in a variety of timber species and are used for feature walls and ceilings. The edges are often veed so that shrinkage gaps are less obvious.

Fascias. Nailed to the ends of the rafters, these dressed and often bullnosed (quarter round) profiles are grooved at the back to take the eave lining (which is usually fibrous cement).

Sidings. Often known as weatherboards, they are available in a variety of profiles (splayed, rusticated, log cabin) and widths. Splayed ones are usually sawn.

Few materials possess the warmth and variety of timber, here used for kitchen cupboards.

Ordering Timber

For small orders, timber is usually sold in linear metres which run in increments of 0.3 of a metre, with the shortest length available being 1.8 m. This means that the sizes will run: 1.8 m, 2.1 m, 2.4 m, 2.7 m, 3.0 m, etc. However, this practice varies with each timber yard and they will often take orders in imperial sizes and sell lengths shorter than 1.8 m.

To check whether you have an orderable length, simply divide the length you want by 3. Say you need a 4.3 m length, 4.3 divided by 3 is uneven so take it up to a measurement that divides exactly by 3: 4.4 doesn't work but 4.5 does. So the length you will have to order and pay for is 4.5 m (this is not really such a waste because the ends of the timber may well have splits and having the bit extra assists you to cut them out).

Keep in mind also that when you order, say, a length 100 x 50 mm, sawn it will end up around 95 mm x 46 mm and, when dressed, 91 mm x 41 mm. You pay for the wastage! Such is life.

Bricks

Used for 7000 years, few products have as much diversity and application as bricks. Ranging from the many-coloured and multi-textured face bricks to common bricks suitable for rendering and use in unseen locations and thence to the ubiquitous pavers, masonry is used extensively in residential construction for structural and feature walls.

Because the basic ingredient is clay, bricks are relatively cheap (although professional laying is not) and supply, except for building boom times, is usually good. Clay, with a little help from other additives, yields an amazing range of colours from white and yellow, through all the pinks, reds and light to dark browns to the clinkers, which are almost black.

Baked in kilns at extremely high temperatures, bricks are a virtually indestructible building material, except where exposed to high salt-water inundation, say near coastlines and swimming pools. Specially made bricks should be used in those situations.

Brickwork, assuming it has been properly manufactured, relies for its strength on four things:

- A good underlying foundation, one that is consistent throughout and, ideally, stable (clay, for example, is often a problem).
- A good concrete footing, one that is of adequate dimensions and properly reinforced.
- High quality laying using a properly proportioned and well-mixed mortar.
- Room to expand (bricks grow over time as each bone-dry unit gradually absorbs moisture).

Brickwork requires little or no maintenance and, if the colour or texture becomes dated, it can be successfully stuccoed, rendered and painted, or merely painted.

Ordering Bricks

There are approximately 48 bricks per square metre in standard single skin, stretcher bond brickwork (assuming a 10 mm joint). It is wise to allow for at least 10% wastage to allow for chips and breakages (simply multiply the total by 1.1 if you want to add 10%). This means if you have a wall 5 × 2 m, the number of bricks required will be:

5 × 2 = 10 square metres.
10 times 48 = 480 bricks.
480 times 1.1 = 528 bricks.

If the fence is double thickness (230 mm thick) or cavity brick simply double the number (1056).

A corner in stretcher bond

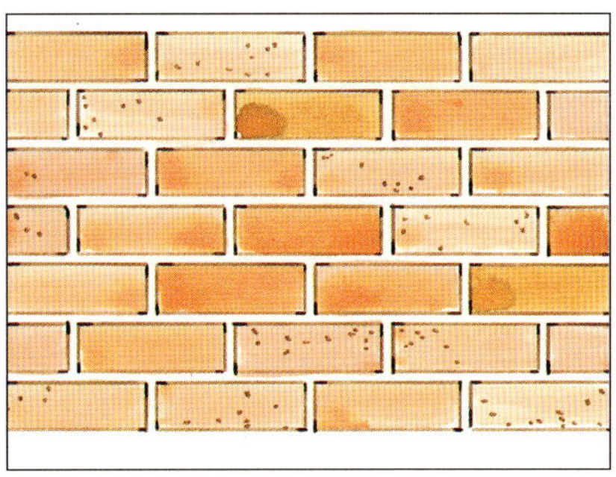

Stretcher bond

Fine brickwork in the wall of a home

Bricks used for paving

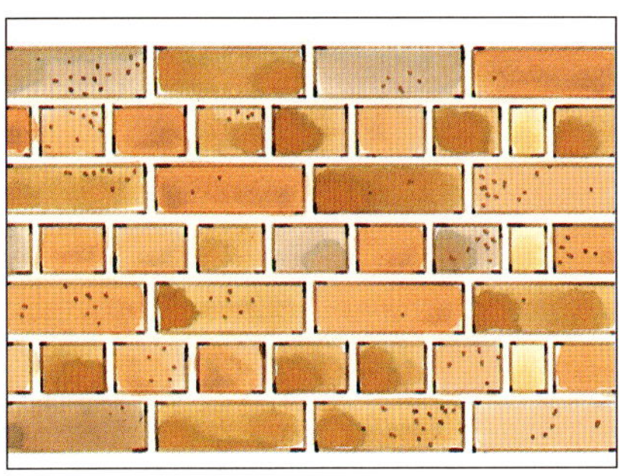

English bond

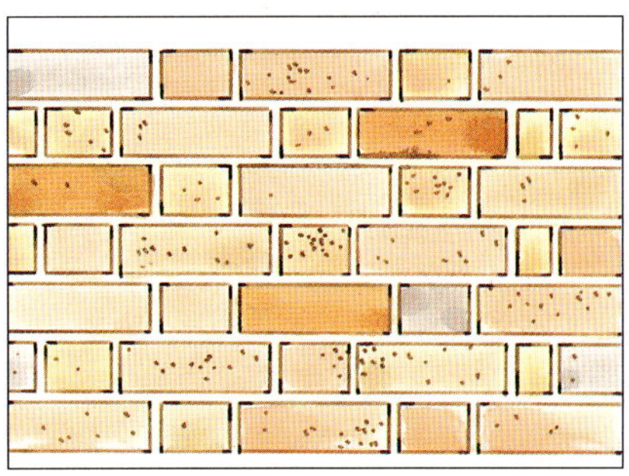

Flemish bond

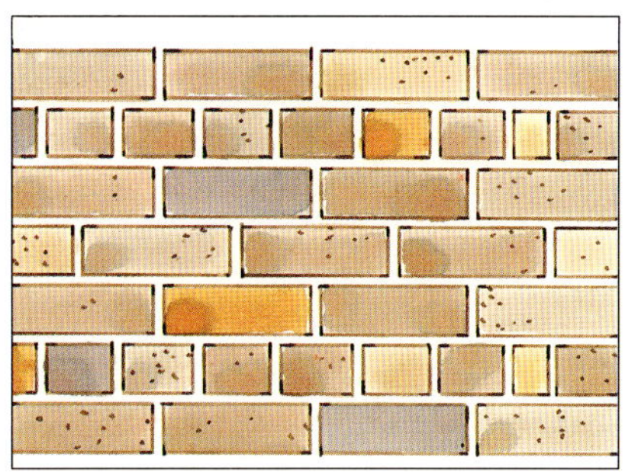

Colonial bond

Building Boards

Building boards, which come in sheets, are made from organic materials combined with various mineral or synthetic ingredients. They are used extensively in home construction for a variety of claddings (the material covering the outside of your house) and linings (materials covering the inside). The products used to make sheet materials are also used to make a variety of tiles, panels, planks, weatherboards, etc.

Because of their diversity, only the main ones will be mentioned and they are presented in terms of softness through to hardness.

Softboard

Once known as Cane-ite because the fibre used was sugar cane, this cheap, low-density building board (now made from radiata pine fibres to which have been added waterproofing agents and binders) has been used for many years as wall and ceiling linings because of its good thermal and fair sound insulating qualities. Another common use is for notice boards. Its soft, pin-absorbing quality comes in part from the light pressing it receives.

It is typically available in sheets of varying thickness (9.5 mm, 12.7 mm, 19.1 mm) and widths (915 mm and 1220 mm). Lengths range from 610 mm up to 3660 mm. It is also manufactured as acoustic tiles and panels.

It should not be used in areas of dampness or where it could be subjected to possible damage (such as children's rooms — there steel plate is best!). It can't be flush-jointed successfully (a batten finish is best but don't forget to leave a 2 mm gap between the sheets to allow for expansion) and won't take wallpaper, but it can be painted or covered with fabrics. Termites love it, but then they also like many other timber products too. Its flammability, unfortunately, is high.

Fixing is achieved by nailing, screwing, stapling or gluing. This should only be done after leaving the sheet exposed to the air for a minimum of 24 hours to allow it to absorb moisture. If gluing, shellac the back of the sheet beforehand to ensure adhesion.

Plywood

This medium-density board, made from thin veneers of timber which are peeled or sliced from logs, then dried and glued together under pressure, is a marvellous material which imparts a warm, natural, non-manufactured look. This contrasts well with the flood of plastic and synthetic products that daily threatens to engulf us.

Because the veneers are laid at right angles to each other, great strength is achieved. The fact that cheaper timbers can be used in the core and/or as a backing, keeps the price down while retaining the expensive timber look (even if the appearance is only skin deep).

Because plywood is, in essence, solid timber, it has good insulating qualities and can be easily worked, fixed and finished with clear or opaque coatings. It is typically available from 3 to 25 mm thick, in widths from 900 to 7500 mm, and lengths from 1800 to 2100 mm. The glue used largely determines where it can be used. Interior quality means just that — don't let water near it! If you are putting ply outside use exterior or marine quality.

Particle Board

This product, which comes in many forms, is basically made from myriad flakes of radiata pine which are glued together with resin, then pressed to make a homogeneous, semi-hard, buff-coloured building board. The flakes near the surface are finer than in the centre, giving a smooth finish.

Particle board, in standard form, is not, I repeat, is *not* waterproof and should never be used where there is any likelihood of it getting wet or damp (say under a kitchen bench or in a bathroom). It absorbs water like blotting paper and then bulges alarmingly while it falls apart.

There are on the market other types of particle board which have varying degrees of moisture resistance. Your supplier, if you describe the situation, will make sure you get the product you need.

Like timber, particle board can be planed, sanded, nailed or screwed, and glued. Unlike timber, it is grainless, which lessens the possibility of splitting and it is equally strong in both directions. But it also means that the edges, being rough textured, are difficult to finish. If exposed, they should preferably be edge-stripped with timber. Particle board shelving can be bought already edge-stripped. Alternatively, you can buy particle board shelving already covered on both faces and one edge with a thin layer of laminated plastic.

Sheet sizes typically range from 1500 × 900 mm up to a whopping 3600 × 1200. Thicknesses start at 10 mm, then move to 13 mm, 16 mm, 18 mm, 25 mm, 33 mm and finish at 43 mm.

There is on the market a better quality particle board (Customwood) which, because the wood chips are reduced into individual fibres before the resins and emulsions are added, yields a more finely textured and easily worked panel board with no edge problems. Mouldings such as skirting and architraves are also made from this excellent product.

An effective use of painted wallboard with a timber profile.

Gypsum Plaster

This versatile lining board has largely replaced the old fibrous plaster of yesteryear. Made from a hard core of calcined gypsum which is faced on both sides with a layer of paper, it gives a relatively strong, non-combustible, sound reducing, vermin-proof lining which can be used for walls, ceilings, etc.

Its flexibility allows it to be curved and the surface, if properly prepared, will take most decorative finishes. For wet or humid areas such as bathrooms and laundries, a special water-resistant type of gypsum plasterboard has been developed. This plasterboard can be successfully tiled over.

Gypsum plaster is typically sold in sheets 1200 mm and 1350 mm wide and either 10 mm or 13 mm thick. Standard lengths range from 2400 mm up to 6000 mm. It is important to select the right edge finish. Order recessed edges if you want an invisible joint. The slightly tapered edge makes room for the jointing material and reinforcement, hence disguising the unsightly bulge.

Square edge, usually applied vertically, requires a moulding finish whereas bevelled edge permanently shows a vee-joint. Both of these types are mainly used in commercial work. You can also get a foil-backed version which provides extra insulation as well as creating a vapour barrier (stops water vapour from penetrating into the wall cavity).

Fixing of gypsum plaster sheets is usually achieved either by galvanised clouts, or adhesive, or a combination thereof. Screws are also used and are considered a superior fastener to nails.

Fibre Cement

Using cellulose fibres to replace the extremely hazardous asbestos fibre, this product, known colloquially as 'fibro', has many applications. It comes in sheet form as a lining for water-prone areas, in thick, dense sheets for flooring to wet areas (compressed fibre cement), and in a variety of weatherboard and planked profiles for cladding. Because of the cement content, it has many of the qualities of concrete (hard, durable, fire resistant, termite proof), but, because of the cellulose reinforcing, it is flexible and light in weight.

It is normally nailed to the framing with galvanised flat-head nails (see Fasteners) which are lightly punched and then filled.

Hardboard

High-density wood fibre board, commonly known as hardboard, has many internal lining and external cladding applications around your home. It is made from Australian hardwood which has been reduced to a fine fibre-like consistency. It is impregnated with synthetic resins before being subjected to high heat and pressure.

It is this high heat that, like bricks, dries the product out completely. Twenty-four hours before use, therefore, the back of the sheets should be thoroughly wet so that the initial expansion can take place. If this isn't done, the sheet will gradually absorb moisture from the air and expand on the wall causing buckling or even popping. A gap of nearly 2 mm should be left between sheets and 6 mm between where the sheet meets the floor, walls or ceilings to allow for further expansion.

It comes in sheets (both standard and the more water-resistant and harder 'tempered' type) which have a variety of surface finishes (smooth, timber-grained, sawn, etc.). Sheet sizes, a standard 4.8 mm thick, range from 1220 mm and 1372 mm wide and from 1830 mm up to 3600 mm long. It is also available in weatherboard profiles and as flooring underlay.

Hardboard can be sawn, planed, sandpapered and nailed like normal timber. Joints can be veed, battened or moulded (using PVC or aluminium moulds). Recommended nails should be cadmium-plated and have slightly flattened heads which may be punched and filled.

If painting, seal with approved wallboard sealer first, and then finish with two coats of paint.

Laminates

Plastic laminates are wonderful products that have many uses. They are made from special papers that have been impregnated with resins, then covered with either a melamine-impregnated colour or a printed design paper with a facing of melamine, before being subjected to high heat and pressure.

They come in an amazing variety of colours, textures and patterns. By varying the core and the thickness of the melamine-impregnated surface, the sheets can be used for thin facings or on curved surfaces (0.8 mm), or for hard-wearing bench tops (1.2 mm), or, if 3 mm thick, for unbacked panels which can be used in bathrooms instead of traditional ceramic tiling. By varying the composition solid colours can be achieved, which means that scratches won't show or can be polished out. Changing the chemicals used can also yield surfaces that are static, burn and chemical resistant.

Plastic laminate used to great effect in a kitchen

Laminates come in sheets, panels, or in edging strips. The latter are useful for the do-it-yourselfer who is involved in laminating new work or re-laminating (covering old bench tops and doors with new, up-to-date laminate). Regardless of the form it comes in, it should be carefully handled to avoid cracking or scratching.

Laminates can be cut with a fine, sharp saw or heavily scored with a tungsten-tipped laminate cutter and then laid over a straight edge and bent away from the cut. The edges can be finished with a plane (or file) although for a large job an electric laminate trimmer is handy.

Plastic laminate is usually fixed by gluing with contact glue (the most popular because it grips immediately and pulls the laminate flat) or PVA (which requires a weight to be applied for several hours). The subsurface is most often particle board (use a moisture-resistant one if water or steam is present) or medium-density fibre board.

Plastic laminate should never be cleaned with powder cleaners.

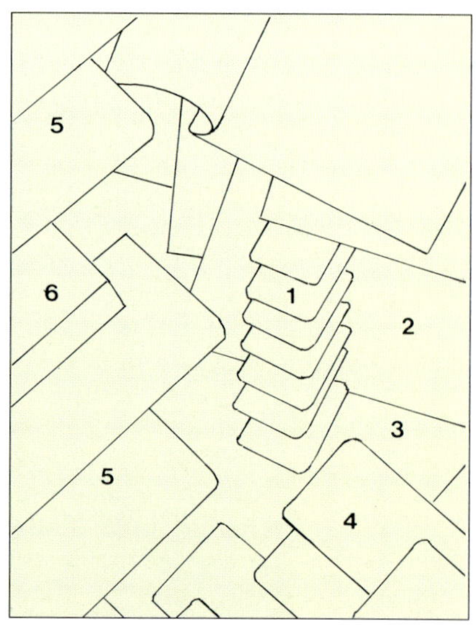

Plastic laminates
1. *Textures and colours imitating natural materials*
2. *and 3. Leathergrain textures*
4. *Printed designs*
5. *Curved edge profiles*
6. *Square edge profile*

Glass

For more than 5000 years, people have known how to make glass. The Egyptians were among the first to make an industry out of it. Though the basic materials haven't changed much, the manufacturing processes have been greatly improved and refined.

The main ingredient is silica which surprisingly is just sand! Other additives include limestone, soda ash and sodium sulphate. Heating the sand mixture up to around 1500°C causes it to melt. In this state it can be blown, spun, drawn, rolled or floated (in a tank of molten tin). The last is now the most common method for making flat glass.

Regardless of the process, the result is a transparent, hard-surfaced, glossy, semi-solid liquid. (Did you know that a pane of glass in time becomes thicker at the bottom than the top?)

The important thing is to get the right glass in the intended position. For example, in high wind areas, glass must be a certain thickness otherwise it may implode (explode inwardly). For access doors, or where a window may be mistaken for an access door, it must by law be laminated safety glass (in case someone runs into it).

Distortion-free glass used in large picture windows should be float (this has largely replaced polished glass). Bathroom and toilet windows should be glazed in patterned or rolled glass which lets in light but not prying eyes. Items such as glass shower screens should be wired or laminated for safety. In areas subject to severe sunlight, heat-absorbent or light and heat reflecting glass can be of great benefit assuming the increased cost can be justified.

If you're going to do some reglazing, the supplier will know what is required assuming you tell him or her where the glass is to be used. When dealing with glass be careful. It's a semi-liquid that cuts!

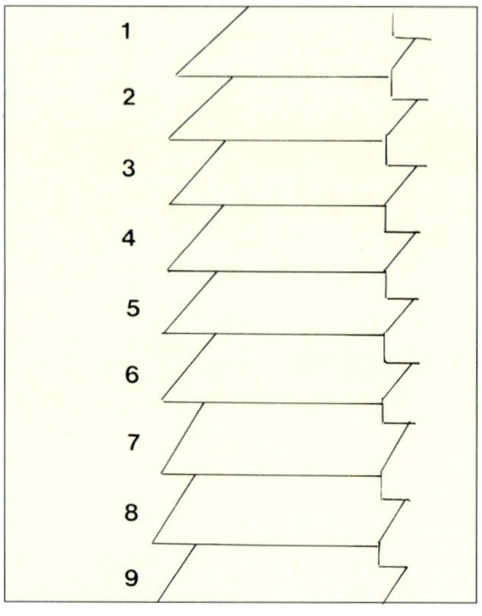

Patterned and wired glass, 3 and 5 mm
1. Clear ribbed
2. Smoked ribbed
3. Square wired, clear
4. Smoked textured
5. Clear textured
6. Rough-textured clear
7. Smoked dimpled
8. Irregularly textured clear
9. Flecked smoked

Concrete

Next to masonry, concrete is one of the oldest building materials, having first been used by the Romans, who used crushed shells (lime) as a binder. Its modern form consists of three basic components: coarse aggregate (gravel), fine aggregate (sand) and a binding agent (cement). When mixed with water, the binding agent generates a chemical reaction which turns it into a powerful 'mineral glue', one which bonds the aggregates together. Concrete, once it has set, continues to gain in strength throughout its life. Its main strength is obtained in 28 days.

The secret to achieving good, strong concrete involves three things.

1. Clean, well-shaped and proportioned aggregates.

A well-shaped aggregate is one with sharp edges (say from crushed material like gravel). Sand should have a mixture of both fine and coarse particles to help fill up the voids between the gravel, hence avoiding thick concentrations of the cement glue which otherwise tends to shrink and crack.

2. Proper measuring and mixing of the dry materials.

Like a cake, maintaining the correct balance of ingredients is essential for good results. For small jobs, bags of pre-mixed concrete are available. For larger jobs, say to 2 cubic metres (over this it is better to order ready-mix), use a volume measure such as a cut-down drum or steel bucket. Mix on a surface that is impervious. A wheelbarrow or concrete mixer is ideal.

If you are mixing it yourself keep in mind that a 1:2½:4 mix (which is ideal for paths and driveways) needs 8 bags of cement, ½ cubic metre of sand and 1 cubic metre of metal to make 1 cubic metre of wet concrete.

3. Clean water.

If you can't drink it, don't use it! The water should be added gradually. Use just enough to make the mix workable. Too much severely weakens the concrete.

Once the concrete is mixed, transport it to the required location, taking care not to shake it too much (because the coarse aggregate may separate from the fine). Place it in position slowly and work it well with a shovel and straight edge. This will bring the bubbles to the surface and compact the mix, thus avoiding honeycombing (a series of interconnected holes). As it begins to harden, a steel (for a smooth finish) or wooden (for a gritty one) float should be used.

If you use reinforcing steel, make sure that you maintain 50 mm minimum clearance from the surface of the concrete to the rods, otherwise the steel may rust and explode the concrete.

Don't allow the concrete to dry out too quickly or it may crack. Once the surface has hardened, periodically hose it during daylight hours or cover it with damp cloth, tarpaulins, or plastic for several days, especially in hot weather.

Pour clean water into well in the middle of concrete mix. Use just enough to make the mix workable.

Wheel the concrete mix carefully and pour it slowly from the wheelbarrow.

Paints

A paint has a twofold purpose: to decorate and protect. Since the advent of the do-it-yourselfer, great progress has been made in producing paints that are easy to apply, long-lasting, and available in a great variety of colours and finishes. The relative cheapness of paint and the startling effect that a new coat of paint can create make it a product that is a boon to the homemaker.

While there is a great deal of information available about paint technology, I'm sure you don't really want to know more than which paint to use on what surface and how to put it on correctly so it will stay there. Later sections tell you how to go about painting a room and rejuvenating the outside of your property.

There are three major types of surface coatings.

Resin-based

Commonly called plastic paints, resin-based paints are made from vinyl, acrylic or polyvinyl acetate (PVA) resins. These paints are water soluble, quick drying, easy to apply, have little odour, and are long lasting. Unlike oil-based paints, they tend to go powdery with age rather than dry out and crack which makes recoating much easier (you don't have to burn or scrape off the old surface as you do with badly deteriorated oil-based paints).

Oil-based

These solvent-borne paints are thinned with mineral turpentine and dry to a hard 'enamel' finish. While the finish is very durable inside a house, unless an exterior surface is frequently recoated the oil can dry out, which can result in blistering, cracking and peeling paint. They are in the main harder to put on, have strong fumes, and cleaning brushes is more difficult.

Polyurethanes

These tough paints are synthetic (a polymer of urethane for the inquisitive), easy to apply and long-lasting.

Before you select a paint, keep in mind where it is going. As a general rule use exterior-type paints wherever the situation is exposed to sun and weather or where extremes of moisture and steam exist (bathrooms, etc.). Elsewhere use the cheaper interior quality paint.

Achieving Good Results

The stability of the home you live in depends to a large extent on having a good foundation. Similarly, the final success of painting depends on the foundation surface, its careful preparation, and the underlying layers of paint supporting the finishing coats. These layers (primers, sealers and undercoats) are often made from the same basic ingredients listed above in paint types but are specially formulated to provide a sound base.

Primers. Oil-based primers penetrate porous surfaces such as are found in timber and other wood products, thereby providing a good key for subsequent layers. Special primers are used for metals.

Sealers. They are used on porous surfaces such as brick, gypsum board and render and are usually plastic-based. They penetrate and seal off the surface.

Undercoats. They are the bridging medium between the primer or sealer and the finish coat. With some plastic paints, the undercoat and final coat are the same.

Finish coats. As the name implies, these are the final coats which impart the colour, surface texture, and sheen (flat, matt, low sheen, semi-gloss and gloss).

Typical Combinations (or Systems)

- Fascias:
  one coat of oil-based primer
  one coat of undercoat (oil-based)
  two coats of enamel.

Or better still

- Fascias:
  one coat of oil-based primer
  two coats of acrylic (semi-gloss or gloss)
- Gypsum Board:
  one coat of sealer (resin-based)
  one coat of undercoat
  one finish coat.

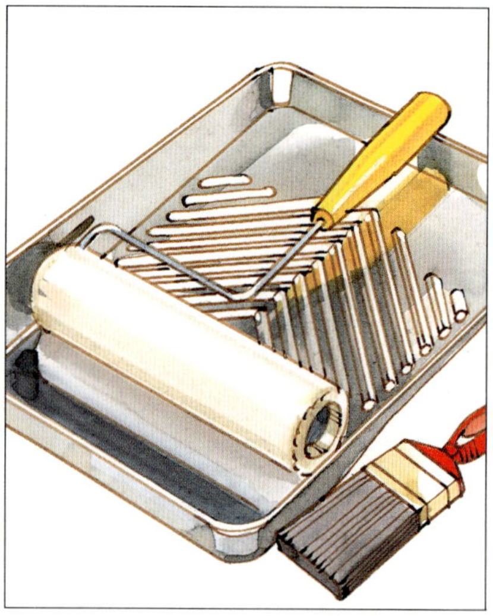

There are many combinations. Make sure when you choose your paint brand and type you read carefully the directions on the can regarding the correct surface preparation and compatible base layers for that product.

Information on surface preparation, painting equipment and techniques is provided in the section on Painting a Room.

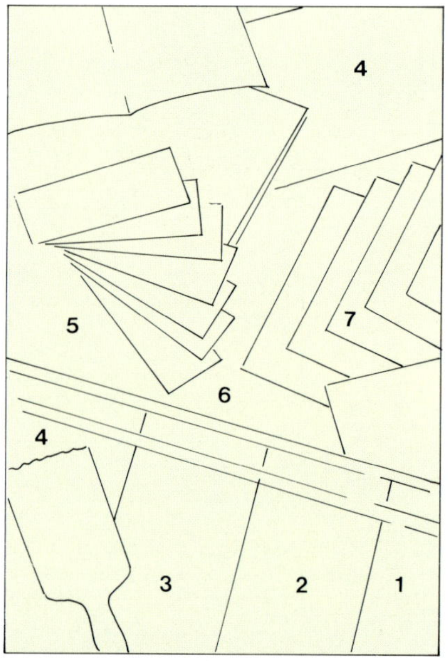

Paint and fabric
1. Raw timber 2. Pink primer
3. Undercoat 4. Enamel gloss finish
5. Semi-gloss enamel 6. Flat acrylic
7. Co-ordinated upholstery fabrics

Fasteners

There is a bewildering array of fasteners on the market. For you, the home handyperson, they may be categorised into three broad groups:

- nails, which are driven with a hammer.
- screws, which are turned with a screwdriver.
- bolts, which usually require a spanner.

Sometimes bolts (and occasionally screws) are used in combination with expanding sleeves, gravity or spring activated toggles and anchors when fixing to masonry or hollow walls.

Keep in mind that for exterior work, hot-dip galvanised fasteners should be used to stop rusting.

Nails

Nails are sold by weight and to order them you should know the length (which must ensure adequate penetration and holding power), the gauge or thickness (to ensure strength), and the head shape (to make sure that the object being nailed is retained).

There are also nails available with special shanks (square, serrated or twisted) to increase their holding power.

For general home maintenance the following types are most commonly used.

Jolt-head. Ranging in length from 15 mm to 150 mm, these general purpose nails can either be left flush with the surface or punched below it and filled.

Flat-head. These come in a variety of head diameters and are used when fixing a softish product (such as fibre boards and plaster) to timber. The bigger head gives better holding power than the jolt-head but cannot be punched as easily or neatly. Common ones are clouts (12 mm to 50 mm), flat-head nails (15 mm to 150 mm) with a serrated head for easy nailing), wallboard nails (15 mm to 25 mm), and fibre cement nails (which have a blunt point to lessen the possibility of splitting).

Panel pin. This fine gauge nail (12 mm to 50 mm) with a small head is excellent for fine joinery and lessens the chance of splitting the timber, especially if nailing near the ends. A hardboard nail is similar to a panel pin but has a diamond-shaped head for an invisible finish.

Screws

Screws, properly installed, have greater holding power than nails but their greatest advantage is that they are easily removed.

Disadvantages are they are more visible, take longer to install, and are more expensive (that's why they are sold by number, not weight).

The major parts of a screw are the head, the shank and the slightly tapered thread. The thread bites into the timber, anchoring itself. Sometimes, for extra strength or for use with metal, the thread is extended right up to the head (e.g. particle board screws and self-tappers).

Screws, like nails, have different heads which relate to the finish required and the material to be fastened. They are recessed to suit the driving system (slot or Phillips head), and are available in a variety of gauges (expressed in numbers) and lengths.

Most screws are made from mild steel (either natural, galvanised, or plated with nickel, zinc, etc.), but, like some nails, are also made in copper, brass, and silicon bronze.

Common types are:

Countersunk. The head of this screw, if the work is recessed with a special bit, can be made flush with the surface.

Raised and round head. A feature is made of this screw head by allowing it to project from the work.

Coach screw. This heavy-gauge screw (25 mm to 200 mm) has a hexagonal head which is turned by a spanner. It is used for heavy jobs like decks and pergolas where strength, not appearance, is the most important factor.

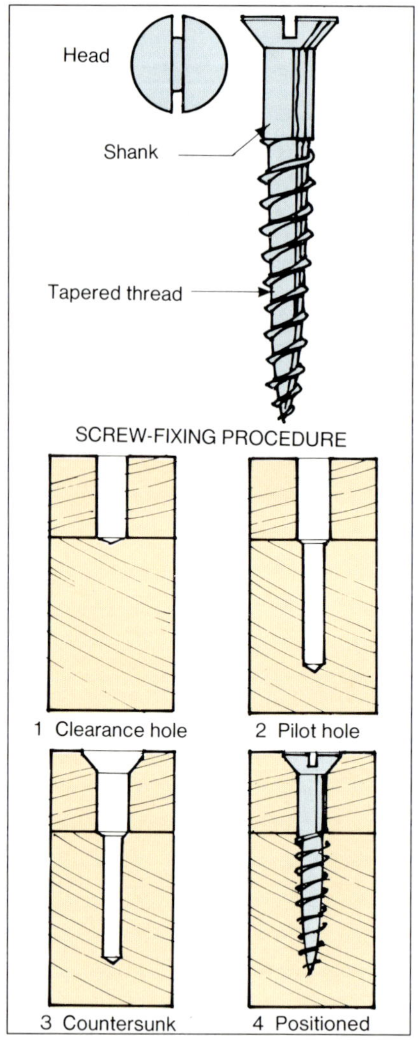

Bolts

Unlike screws, bolts do not cut a thread in the timber or metal but usually project through it and tie into a nut or other threaded material. Unlike screws, the centre core is cylindrical, not tapering, and the threads are much finer. The holding power of bolts in timber can be increased by using suitable washers. The most commonly used types of bolts are:

Hexagon bolts. Available in diameters of 6 to 20 mm and lengths from 20 to 600 mm, hexagon bolts are mainly used for securing heavy timber sections.

Cup bolts. A variation is the round-headed, square-collared cup bolt, which, if the collar grips properly, can be tightened by just turning the nut (no need to hold the head with a spanner). It also gives a slightly neater finish.

Miscellaneous Fasteners

Anchor bolt. A metal or plastic sleeve on the end of the bolt expands to grip concrete, brick or stone around the pre-drilled hole. Diameters range from 6 to 25 mm and lengths from 50 to 300 mm.

Toggles. Using bolts which fit into a threaded toggle, these handy little devices can be poked through a hole in a hollow wall where gravity or springs expand the toggle. Tightening the bolt locks the arms against the back of the hollow material.

Anchors. Using basically the same principle as toggles, they employ a plastic or nylon sleeve to lock the bolt or screw.

Screw hooks and eyes. Used for hanging pictures, etc., these multi-shaped, screw-threaded items can be screwed into timber framing or, in masonry walls, plugs.

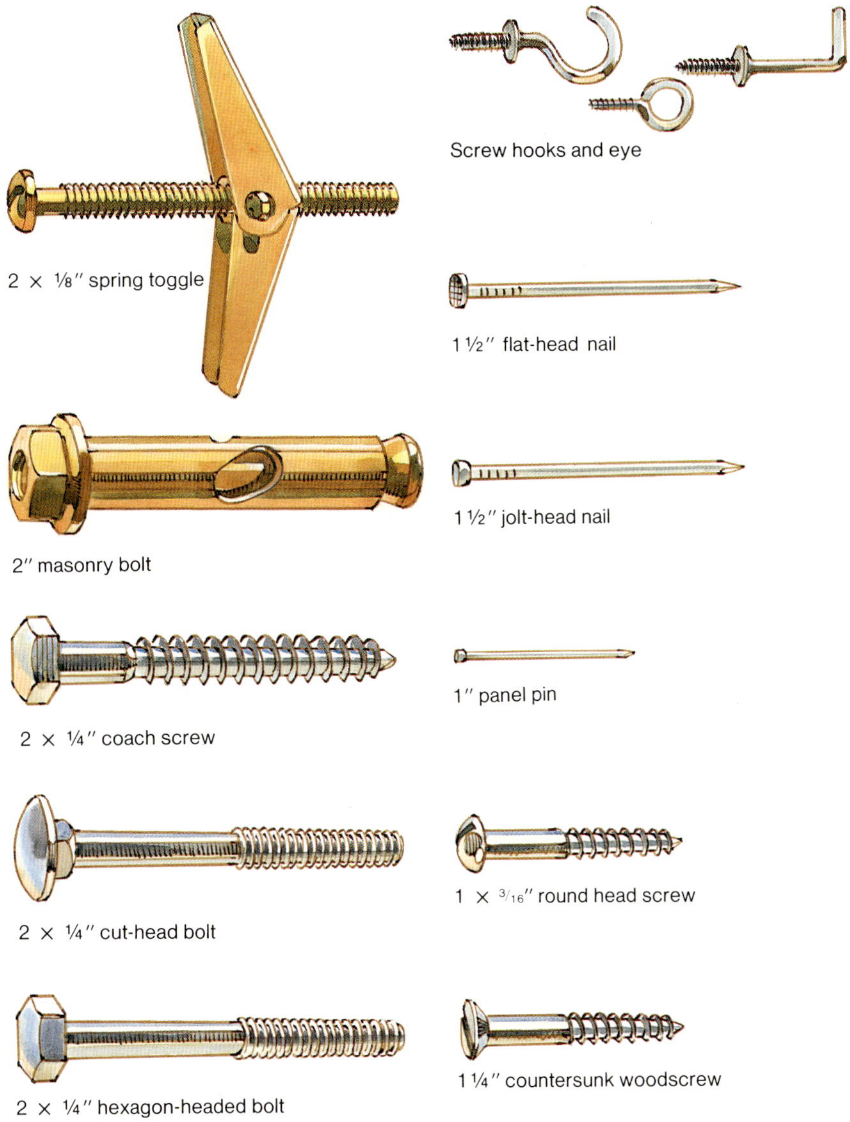

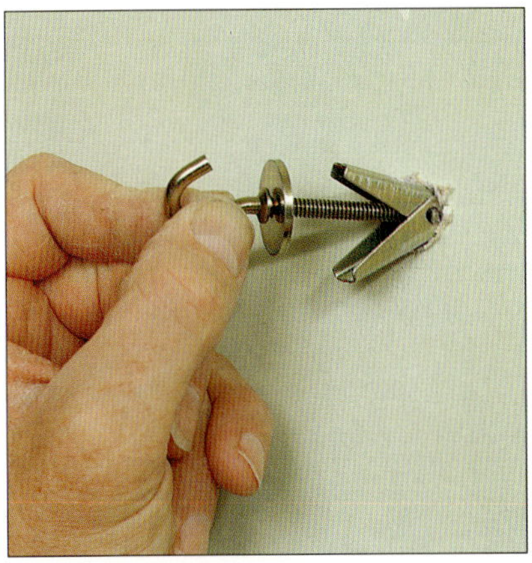

A hook with a spring toggle for use in a hollow wall.

A bolt projects through the timber it is in and ties into a nut.

To pull out a nail use the claw end of a hammer and protect the surface with an odd scrap of wood.

Glues

Glues are products that, used properly, can save you a small fortune by restoring broken and faulty household items to a close replica of their former glory.

Unlike the old days of messy glue pots containing boiled down animal hides, etc., there are now on the market a large number of easily mixed and applied types. I will discuss the three most useful ones (and one minor one) for the home and how they should be used. Remember that they are much cheaper if bought in large amounts.

The rules for preparing any surface for gluing are simple. The surface must be totally clean, dry, and, for best results, roughened slightly with a suitable abrasive paper.

Epoxy Resin

This is the glue with the greatest universal application. Unfortunately, it is also the most expensive. This two-part adhesive can be bought in tubes for small jobs or tins for larger applications. When mixed properly, it sets to a hard finish which is tremendously strong, water-resistant, non-staining, gap-filling, heat-resistant and it sticks to virtually everything (excluding thermoplastics). It is excellent for mending glassware, china, metal, wood, etc. as well as for exterior applications.

It sets quickly (in about one hour depending on the temperature) but for special jobs which don't require great strength you can get one that sets in five minutes (although the strength suffers). However, full strength is not achieved for 24 hours.

When using epoxy, care must be taken to mix equal quantities of each part on an impervious (waterproof) surface. A plastic, glass or ceramic lid is ideal but select one that can be thrown away. After you've squeezed out a line of equal length from each tube (or equal scoops from tins), watch you don't get the container tops mixed or you'll never get them off! Use a paddle-pop stick as a stirrer and mix thoroughly.

Smear the adhesive thinly on both surfaces making sure you don't get the glue on your skin (it can cause dermatitis) or inhale the vapours (they're toxic). Use plastic gloves if it's an awkward job. Compress the surfaces together if possible, using a clamp, or put them between newspapers under a pile of books. Rounded items like the pieces of a teapot or coffee mug can be temporarily held in place with masking tape.

PVA Adhesives

This multi-purpose, non-toxic, one-part, medium strength white glue is cheap and very useful for sticking wood, some plastics (polyvinyls), and paper. It's also easy to wipe off. It's not recommended for use where moisture can get into a joint or where timber staining could be a problem. It's good for fixing wooden toys and for positions where you need a glue to run into a joint (such as in a wobbly table or chair leg). Apply glue liberally to one surface only and clamp surfaces while drying for 12 hours. Wipe off excess glue immediately.

Unlike epoxy, this product does not pose any health hazards.

Contact Glue

This one-part glue is useful for a large number of jobs, but is not ideal for timber joints, glass or ceramics. Its major advantage is that it is self-cramping — once it grips it won't let go! Cheaper than epoxy, it can be used to glue many things (it is especially good for sticking plastic laminate). It lacks the strength of epoxy and is not gap-filling but it remains flexible so it can be used on substances like rubber, leather and textiles.

It is brushed or spread on both surfaces (porous surfaces require two coats) and left until it is touch dry (no longer sticky). Then carefully align the two surfaces and place them together. Bingo! They're stuck. If you're unsure of the alignment, use some plastic or wooden spacers to help you line it up, then gradually withdraw them. Light pressure can assist the bond.

Acrylic Glue

This product, often called Liquid Nails (trade name), is available in tubes or, for large jobs, a cartridge. It can be used for a variety of jobs which involve bonding porous and even damp materials such as timber, plaster, fibrous cement, ceramics, masonry, etc., to each other. Made from acrylic, and looking like brown toothpaste, this adhesive is squeezed on in dobs or beads. The materials to be glued should then be held with temporary fasteners until the adhesive dries. It's handy to have a tube of this versatile product around.

With these glues you can confidently attack most household repairs. For special jobs check with your hardware store or contact the adhesive manufacturers. They happily supply technical information free of charge.

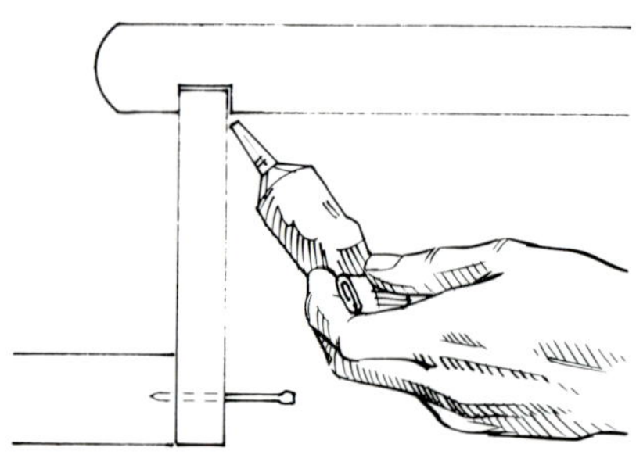

Fillers and Caulkers

Fillers are products that, as the name implies, fill cracks, holes and dents in building materials. Sealants, just as obviously, stop the ingress or egress of water, draughts, odours, etc.

Fillers typically fall into two major categories: oil-moistened and water-moistened. The most common oil-moistened filler is putty. Made from whiting and linseed oil, this useful product can be used to fill smallish holes in timber. It forms a skin on the top that will take paint but will remain soft underneath and won't crack because the oil stops it being totally dried out by the timber. Interestingly, when putty is used for glazing, it becomes a sealant as well as a filler.

Exterior and interior quality water-moistened fillers are often made from cellulose (the main constituent of wood), PVA, acrylic or cement. Mixed to a putty or paste-like consistency (or bought ready-mixed), when applied to cracks in render, plaster, wood etc., they dry to a hard, non-shrinking finish which can be nailed or screwed into and sanded smooth. Large patches should be primed with an oil-based undercoat or sealer.

One of the most useful sealant/caulkers on the market today is made from silicone. It remains flexible, allowing differential movement without cracking. With various additives, it can be applied to most surfaces where it forms a skin in 10 minutes, cures in 24 hours, but shouldn't dry out or crack for two decades! It comes in a translucent colour for a virtually invisible joint as well as grey (for concrete), white (for around baths) and bronze (for brown aluminium windows). Special types can be painted over. Other common sealants have bitumen or butyl rubber bases.

Surfaces to be sealed should be clean, sound (no rust or flaking), fully cured and dry. Silicone joints should ideally be no more than 6 to 12 mm in cross-section.

The Next Step

Well, that completes the section on tools and materials. Now we're ready to attack the jobs armed with the essential knowledge that will help bring the jobs to a successful completion. Are you ready?

Here a hardening wood filler is being used to fill a hole in floorboards. If a hole is too large, glue in a block.

MAIN SW.
KILOWATT HOURS
84785
WATTHOUR METER TYPE B.A.Z.
902485
84785
BRITE-HEAT
FUSE WIRE
USE ONE STRAND

PART TWO

MAINTENANCE PROJECTS

Even if you never undertake changing a single thing or add something as elementary as a towel rack to your home, you will be confronted by one or more common maintenance problems each year. You have a choice: pay for a tradesperson or do it yourself.

If you have always taken refuge in 'I've got no talent for practical things' or 'I didn't do woodwork at school and I'm all fingers and thumbs', then think again. You *can* do these things. We'll do them together — I'll show you how if you'll let me! If you make a little mistake, I won't tell anyone and anyway, who cares? Everyone makes mistakes. Tradesmen make errors all the time. I know — I've taught them for years. That's why they have putty, fillers and glues.

Before undertaking the first job, pick one of your good days when you're not tired or distracted and no friends are likely to call. Wear old clothes but don't be sloppy. Loose clothing can be dangerous. Wear thin gloves if you're worried about your hands and put long hair up out of the way. If you use electric tools make sure someone is around just in case something goes wrong and ALWAYS keep leads away from water.

Arrange the tools and all the materials required neatly in the work area. If there is going to be mess, lay down some old sheets. Cover all surfaces that could be damaged by metal tools, etc., with an old blanket. Remove all Ming vases. Put on some soft music. Read my instructions again over a cup of coffee (several times if necessary) so that you know *beforehand* the general procedure. Read the instructions on all tins, packets and tubes. If everything isn't clear, don't panic. I rarely understand instructions first off. It's the fault of these damned writers who can't explain themselves properly! Approach the problem telling yourself, 'I can do it!' Of course you can.

Don't forget to tidy up. Put your tools away neatly. Check you've cleaned off any excess glue or paint runs that might set and that there aren't any suspicious bits and pieces left on the bench (like a washer that should be in a tap). Then go out and celebrate!

Refastening Loose Hinges or Catches

You've had it! A catch keeps falling off or a hinge keeps loosening because the screws won't hold. You've tried to re-screw them but, when you're not looking, they fall out again. If the screws were holding correctly, the thread on the screw should have cut into the sides of the pilot hole, thereby locking itself in. However, if the screws become overstressed, perhaps because someone has put leverage on the door or the catch is sticking, the timber around the screw thread gives way and the thread has nothing to hold to. Fixing it is easy. Here's how.

Dip matches in glue and hammer them into the old screw holes.

TOOLS AND MATERIALS

A trimming knife, hammer, nail punch, and a screwdriver will do the trick. You will also need some wooden matches and PVA glue.

PROCEDURE FOR HINGES

1 Open the door until it is at right angles to the frame. Then, using some thin books, scraps of timber, or coasters, pack the bottom of the door off the floor. Now when you take out the offending screws, the door will remain level and in its correct position.

2 With your screwdriver pressed hard into the slot, unscrew the loose screws. If the slots are filled with paint, scratch it out with a nail file or pointed knife. Fold the leaf of the hinge back so you can clearly see the holes.

3 Cut the phosphorus off several matches with a knife. Dispose of it in a safe place because it's poisonous. Depending on the hole size, take two or three matches and dip them in the glue, making sure it covers a distance equal to the length of the screws.

4 Hammer the matches tightly into the screw holes. Let them dry (say two hours).

5 With your chisel or a knife, cut the matches off until they're flush with the surface.

6 Using your nail punch and hammer, make pilot holes for the screws in the centre of the plugged holes (otherwise the hinge won't go back in the same place). Drive the punch in at least half the length of the screw.

7 Carefully rescrew the hinge back into position, making sure you tighten the screws fully. If you can get the slots all pointing in a vertical direction, then it will look very tradesperson-like.

8 Take out the packing and close the door. While you're at it, check the clearance margins around the door. If they're uneven you can make them right by either taking a little more out of the hinge recess with a sharp chisel or by packing behind the hinge with a strip of cardboard.

PROCEDURE FOR CATCHES

1 Remove the catch and fill the oversized holes as above. Make the pilot holes.

2 Check another catch to see how it goes on. Put the catch in position and start to turn the screws clockwise. Make sure that you select a screwdriver that fits the screw head properly. If the screws keep falling over, tap them in a little way with your hammer and then screw them in the rest of the way.

3 Close the door slowly and check the catch position. The holes in the catch are often elongated to allow for adjustment. Loosen the screws if necessary, move the catch backwards or forwards until the door fits correctly, then re-tighten the screws.

Congratulations. You did it! When the children, spouse or special friend comes home don't gloat. Perhaps another catch or hinge is plotting an escape.

Cut the matches off to make them flush with the surface.

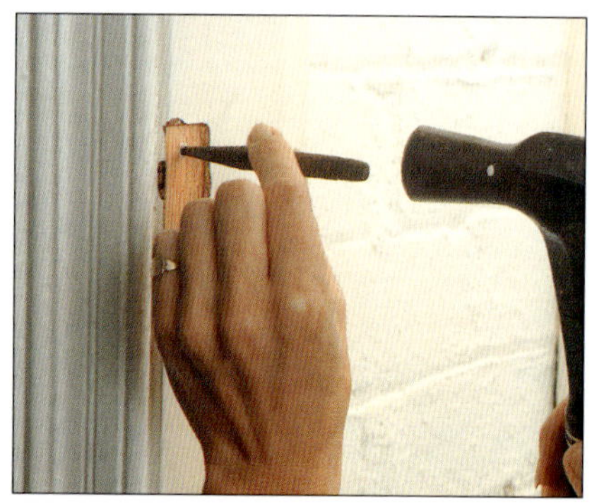

Use a nail punch to make pilot holes for the screws.

Rescrew the hinge into position, tightening the screws fully.

Replacing a Fuse Wire

There's nothing worse than being home alone at night and suddenly the lights go out. Or the television goes off in the middle of a movie.

Assuming there isn't a blackout, it could just mean a *replaceable* fuse has gone. This fuse is a thin piece of wire which is designed to melt in the event of an electricity overload caused by a faulty appliance or poor wiring. This melting breaks the power circuit. If the fuse weren't there you'd probably have a fire.

Fixing a fuse is easy providing you prepare for it *before* it happens.

The Meter Box

The first thing to do is to find the meter box. For a house it is usually a steel box with a door located on an outside wall. In the case of units, it will usually be in a special meter room along with everyone else's. In all situations it must be accessible to the meter readers.

Once you find it, open the door and prop it up. Typically you will see various dials and a series of white porcelain fuse-holders which are labelled lights, power points, stove, etc. You will also find a main switch which turns off the power supply to the house and perhaps a separate switch for the hot water.

Turn off the main switch and gently pull out one of the fuse-holders. You will see a thin piece of wire stretched between its two ends. If a fuse has blown this piece of wire will be melted; if it's faulty, it will be broken. The wire is fixed at both ends by screws. Just undo the screws, pull the old wire out and replace it with the new. BUT YOU MUST REPLACE IT WITH THE SAME GAUGE WIRE!

If you use a thinner wire it will burn through too easily and if you use too thick a wire it won't burn through when it should, hence potentially setting the electrical wiring in your home on fire. Often the correct gauge (thickness) required is stamped onto the fuse holder.

Make sure you put each fuse holder back in the right place because different circuits require different gauges. Generally, lighting needs 8 amp wire and power needs 15 amp wire. A 3.6 kilowatt hot water system needs 15 amp, while a 4.8 kilowatt hot water system needs 20 amp. Electric stoves require either 20 or 30 amp wire. Check with your supply authority for requirements.

Now you know how it works, put the fuse back, switch on the main switch, and close the meter box.

Pull out the fuseholders one at a time to locate the broken wire.

Undo the screws and remove the pieces of wire.

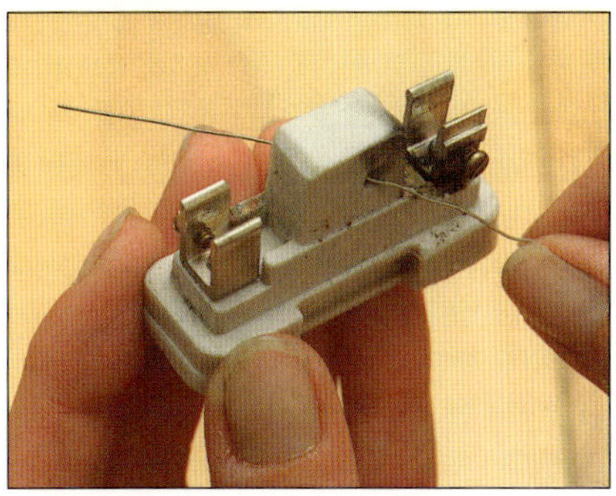

Replace the fuse using wire of the same gauge.

Wrap the ends of the wire clockwise round the retaining screws.

TOOLS AND MATERIALS

Buy a selection of different gauge fuse wires, a torch, and a small screwdriver. Keep them in a place that can be found in the dark.

PROCEDURE

1 First, look outside to see if there is a general blackout. If it's daylight, check other appliances or ring a neighbour.

2 If only your house is affected, collect your fuse kit and make your way to the meter box.

3 Switch off the main switch. This is very important.

4 Check the porcelain fuse-holders one at a time. Replace each fuse until you locate the one with the molten or broken wire.

5 Undo the screws, remove the pieces, and replace the fuse using wire of a similar gauge. Wrap the ends of the wire in a clockwise direction around the retaining screws.

6 Tighten the screws and cut off any loose ends of wire. Replace the fuse-holder and switch on the main power.

7 If the lights or power fuses blow again try to establish the cause of the overload. If an appliance appears to be faulty, disconnect it. If you have a number of double adaptors banked up, remove them. Then do the fuse again.

If it still blows, call an electrician or your electricity supply authority. The latter may be willing to come and investigate.

Fixing Squeaky Stairs and Floors

Squeaking stairs or floorboards can create unnecessary discords in your life. They are fairly easily fixed. Let's go!

Squeaky Stairs

This is usually caused by movement taking place between where the riser joins the treads either at the top or bottom. Diagram 1 shows the usual places. Position yourself behind the stairs and get someone to walk on them until you locate where the problem is. Mark the spot with a pencil.

To solve the problem you can use either nails or glue. If you decide on nailing and the squeak is coming from the top of the riser, drive in 50 mm nails 150 mm apart through the top of the tread and into the riser and punch the heads below the surface. If the squeak is coming from the bottom of the riser, from under the stairs, nail through the bottom of the riser into the back of the tread.

As an alternative to nailing, squeeze some wood glue into the joints and allow to set for twenty-four hours before walking on the stairs. If you really want to be sure, glue *and* nail the offending joints.

Squeaky Floorboards

This is usually caused by movement between the boards and is most often due to shrinkage. First, try sprinkling some talcum powder into the offending joint. If this doesn't work, to permanently stop the movement locate the general area and, if there is room, get under the house and have someone tread about until you spot the squeaky joint.

If it's occurring *over a joist* then measure its position and direction by measuring off the foundation walls or count how many boards it is away from the wall plate. Carefully mark its position from above, then renail and punch the nails down. (See Diagram 2.) If there is carpet you can nail straight through the carpet provided you can accurately locate the position (but don't forget to punch the nails down).

In either case, turn the nails over and flatten the points BEFORE you drive them in — taking the point off the nail minimises the wedging effect and helps to stop the boards splitting.

If the squeak is coming from an area of flooring *between the joists*, screw in some 18 mm screws from underneath the floor. Space them every 100 mm or so along the offending join. Be careful not to sink the screws in too far or they'll project beyond the top of the boards. If you're unlucky, the noise may be coming from several places so be sure you cover them all.

If the squeaks are coming from an upstairs room and you can't get to the joints from underneath because of a ceiling, then lift the carpet where the squeak is and either renail the joints or screw down between them from the top. As an alternative, squeeze some wood glue into the joints between the boards and allow to dry. Then refix the carpet making sure you stretch it tightly. (If you have squeaks in particle board floors the same general principles apply.)

Now turn on the stereo and listen to your favourite records or plan to come home late. The only squeaks will be from mice!

1

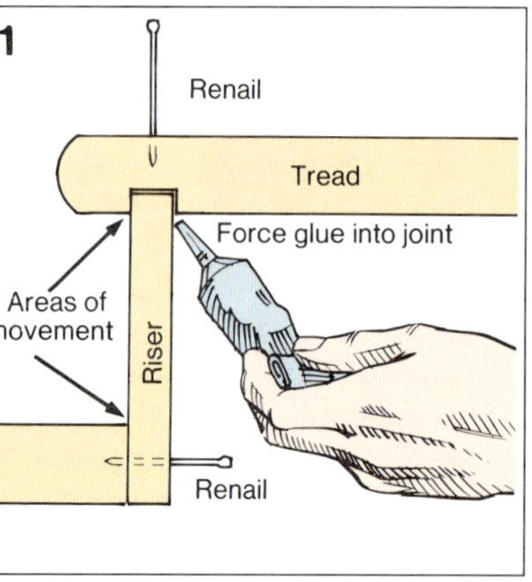

2

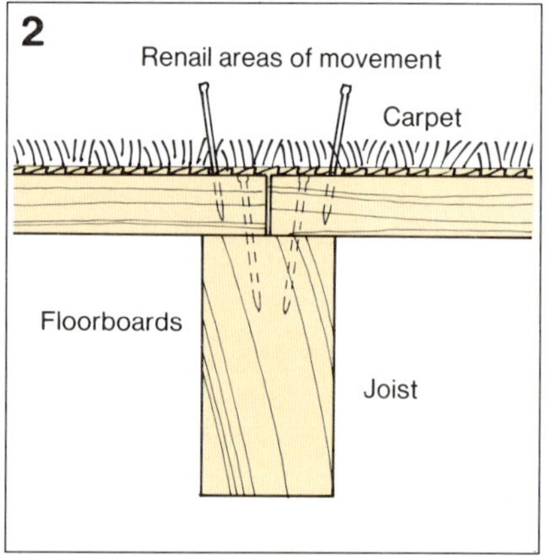

Rectifying Sticking Doors

Sticking doors can be annoying. The sticking sometimes occurs because the screws, being too small or put in incorrectly, become overstressed and partly pull out of the timber. It can also be caused by a build-up of paint narrowing the necessary gap between the door and the frame (the jamb). Another possibility is that moisture is getting into the door and making it swell.

The solutions to all three problems are easy.

Loose Screws

To establish if this is the problem open the door 100 mm and, using your arms, pull and push it towards the hinges. If there is movement then the screws are loose in either the door or the jamb. A telltale sign is cracked paint around the hinge.

To fix loose screws see Refastening Loose Hinges or Catches.

A Swelling Door

Keep an eye on whether the door sticks in humid weather or when the room is subjected to a lot of steam. If so, this means that moisture is getting into the timber through the joints or unpainted surfaces and causing it to swell. Not only does this cause sticking but long term it can lead to rotting. It may also cause the door to come apart because the glue gives way.

Wait for an extended period of dry weather or until you return from a holiday. If the door is no longer sticking, take it off and paint any areas that are bare or cracked. Pay careful attention to the top and bottom of the door and any joints that show hairline cracks. By sealing the door fully you stop any moisture entering the timber, which should end the problem forever.

With sandpaper wrapped round a block, sand the offending area.

Removing Built-up Paint

The solution to this problem depends on the thickness of the build-up and the area of contact between the door and the jamb. If the whole edge of the door is sticking badly you may have to get in a carpenter to plane the door unless you have a plane and know how to use it (see Hand Tools and later in this topic). For small areas the following procedure is suitable.

TOOLS AND MATERIALS

Screwdriver, cork block, pencil and rule; sandpaper (both rough and fine) and suitable paint.

SANDING PROCEDURE

1 Check where it's sticking. When you are finished there should be an even 2 mm gap to allow for clearance after repainting. Using a pencil, mark how much of the sticking area you need to sand off. Remove the door if it's binding on the hinge side or on the bottom, otherwise sand it in position.

2 Using the rough sandpaper and the block, heavily sand the offending area. Make sure you keep the block flat and slightly angled towards the back of the door (the surface that fits in the rebate). Finish it off with the fine sandpaper. Then use the sandpaper to take the sharp edge off the corners. This is called arrissing and is done to stop splintering and to give the door a neat finish.

3 Screw the door back on (if necessary) and check the gap for evenness and size. Sand further if required, prime and repaint the door.

PLANING PROCEDURE

1 If the whole edge is sticking and you have a plane, mark the 2–3 mm clearance, take the door out of the frame (either by taking out all the screws from the jamb or, if the hinge has a loose pin, driving the pin up with a hammer and a 75 mm nail).

2 Next, set the plane iron. This involves firstly using the depth adjustment knob to wind the sharp blade (see Hand Tools for parts) out say 0.5 to 0.75 mm beyond the sole (bottom) of the plane. Next, hold the plane up towards the light and, using the lateral adjusting lever, make the blade parallel with the sole.

3 Get a friend to hold the door or push it into the corner of a room. If you're planing on the lock side you will have to remove the lock.

When planing, start with the weight on the front of the plane. As you come off the timber, transfer the weight to the back. This will ensure the timber stays straight. If it's too hard to push, wind the blade back in. If lines appear on the timber, the blade is digging in on one side. Check it again for parallel.

If the wood is tearing you may be planing against the grain. Try planing from the opposite direction. If it tears from both directions, it has 'cranky' grain. Plane the way it tears the least.

4 Make sure you slightly undercut the edge towards the back of the door. Arris the corners to get rid of sharp edges. Then screw the door back in the jamb, check the clearance, and repaint all bare surfaces.

Replacing a Tap Washer

Given that up to 50% of an electricity bill may be attributable to water heating, it is important to ensure that your hot water taps don't drip. Did you realise that up to 45 litres of water per day can flow from each dripping tap? That's money down the drain! Another problem with a dripping tap that is left for too long is that the water may badly stain the surface of a basin or bath.

A leaky tap usually occurs because the internal washer that creates a watertight seal is worn out. Each time you turn the tap off, the soft flexible washer, which is made from rubber or a synthetic substitute, presses against the metal washer seat, wearing a tiny part of itself away. Eventually it becomes thin and irregular in shape. This allows water to seep past and creates the annoying drip.

If you don't replace it but continue to screw the tap down tighter and tighter, eventually you will get metal grinding against metal which will force you to call in a plumber to regrind the washer seating. That can be an expensive business!

Before you attempt the job, first check with your local water supply authorities to make sure you can change the washers.

The reason the water supply authorities have such strict rules concerning plumbing and drainage and insist generally that all work is carried out by a licensed plumber is that they don't want the water supply contaminated by faulty work. You could imagine the health risk if some foreign substance or bacteria got into the water pipes or the drainage system was interfered with.

Before beginning the job of replacing a tap washer, turn off the water supply at the mains tap next to the meter.

Lift the hot or cold button and undo the screw underneath.

Lift off or unscrew the cover or flange of the tap.

Unscrew the hexagonal collar with an adjustable spanner.

The offending washer is fixed to the jumper by a small nut.

Using pliers to hold the jumper, undo the nut with the spanner.

Slip the jumper with the new washer back into position.

To finish the job rescrew the whole assembly back into position.

TOOLS AND MATERIALS

A screwdriver, a large adjustable spanner or wrench, pliers, the correct sized washer (18 mm for most bath and mixer taps and 12 mm for others) and an old towel. You can buy disposable plastic jumpers with washers attached.

PROCEDURE

1 Turn off the water supply to the offending tap. This may be done by:

(a) turning off the main water supply near the meter, or

(b) turning off the supply stop cock (if there is one) beneath the sink or basin, etc.

Note. In the case of a roof-mounted hot water storage system or a hot water system that supplies a tap underneath a house, turn off the supply at the heater (otherwise all the water may run out, which could cause damage to the unit).

2 Turn the tap full on. If you have successfully turned off the supply, the water should quickly stop running. If it doesn't, check the cocks again, remembering you must turn the handle *clockwise*.

3 Put the old towel in the sink. If you drop something it lessens the chance of damage.

4 Remove the tap handle. This is done by undoing the screw at the side or lifting the hot or cold indicator button and undoing the screw underneath. Take the handle off, and then lift off or unscrew the cover or flange. Lay them both on the sink.

5 You will see the mechanism of the tap exposed. Set the adjustable spanner to the size of the large hexagonal-shaped collar and unscrew it in an anti-clockwise direction. Remove the assembly.

6 You will find the offending washer (fixed to the jumper by a small nut) either in the bottom of the tap (a pair of tweezers could be handy here) or in the end of the assembly you've just removed.

7 Using the pliers to hold the jumper, undo the nut with the spanner, remove the old washer and, checking it is the same size, put the new one in its place and retighten the nut (but not excessively otherwise you'll distort the washer).

8 Check there are no pieces of the old washer left on the seating, then slip the jumper back into its position and firmly rescrew the whole assembly back into place (making sure the jumper body fits into the hole at the end of the assembly). Also make sure that the tap handle is left in its full-on position.

9 Then put back the cover and the tap handle. Turn the tap off and, with someone watching, slowly turn the supply back on. If it runs, either you've put the assembly back incorrectly or you've used the wrong sized washer. Recheck.

If the drip has stopped, feel proud. You have accomplished something new and perhaps saved yourself excess heating and water bills.

If it still drips there must be damage to the seating and unfortunately you'll have to call in a plumber.

If you are particularly adventurous, you could try reseating the washer yourself, using a reseating tool which can be obtained from hardware stores. If you need a plumber, make sure you get at least four quotes.

Rehanging a Picture

Rehanging a picture (or framed mirror) of any size involves putting up fastenings that must be fixed so securely that they will never pull out of the wall (thus damaging your favourite Monet!). When selecting fasteners, keep in mind the weight that has to be supported. It may be better to use two or even three fasteners for a painting that is extra large or has a heavy frame.

Positioning the Picture

This operation is easier with two people. Get someone to hold the painting so you can stand back and position it to its best advantage. Don't hurry! Wear out two or three friends if necessary. When it's just right, lightly mark where the top and both sides of the frame touch the wall with a soft pencil. Then lay the frame down, pull the wire or chain tight (towards the top), and mark where the fastener(s) should go (see photograph). Measuring from your wall markings, accurately transfer these marks.

After positioning, lightly mark where the top and sides of the picture touch the wall.

Pull the wire tight and mark where the fastener should go.

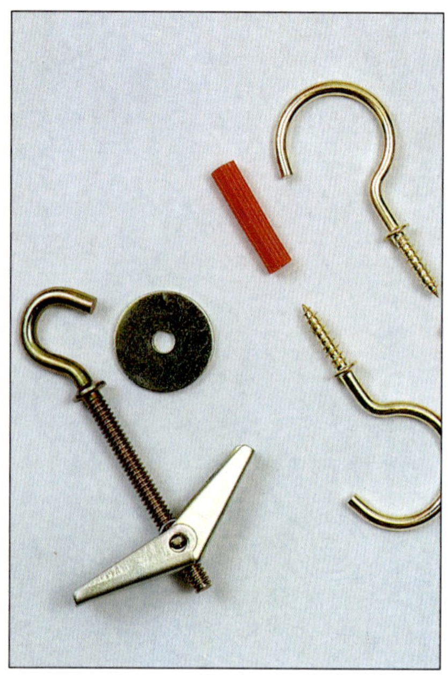

Brass hooks, a wall plug and a hook with a toggle.

TOOLS AND MATERIALS
For masonry walls you will need a 6 mm masonry drill bit plus electric or hand drill, plugs (either plastic or timber), tape and pencil.

For timber frame walls you will need a hammer, tape and pencil, pliers, and a thin nail. If there is no wall framing where the hook is to go, you'll also need an electric or hand drill plus a drill bit to suit the hook / toggle diameter.

A popular fastener is the screw hook or screw eye. Both have a threaded screw section combined with either a hook or an open eye (see Fasteners). They are made from brass or steel and, if visible, are available in special finishes.

For masonry walls, make sure the thread is at least 15 mm long; where solid fixing is available in timber frame walls, the minimum thread length should be 25 mm (to allow for the 10 mm lining thickness). For hollow walls, a brilliant innovation is a hook which screws into a toggle (see photograph).

PROCEDURE FOR MASONRY WALLS
To provide good fixing you must drill a hole in the masonry and then fill it with a material that the threaded fastener can screw into. Make sure you drill the hole 2 mm deeper than the thread length of the fastener. The hole can then be plugged with a soft timber such as cedar or maple (use a chisel or trimming knife to shape a plug slightly larger than the hole, then hammer it in). Alternatively you can use a plastic plug the same diameter as the drill (see photograph).

Screw the hook or eye into the plug with pliers until the shoulder hits or the thread disappears.

PROCEDURE FOR TIMBER FRAME WALLS

There are two options.

1 If the exact location is not essential, fix into the nearest timber stud. Position the painting as before, then tap along the wall with a hammer in the vicinity of the marks. Where the wall sounds most solid, drive in a thin nail to check if you've located a stud (watch you don't hit any plumbing or electric wiring). Then screw in the fastening. Should two hooks be necessary you'll usually find another stud either 450 mm or 600 mm either side of the first.

2 If positioning is vital and there are no studs, use the hook / toggle. Drill a hole the diameter of the toggle through the wall lining in the exact position, then push the toggle into the hole until the arms open by gravity or spring. As you continue to tighten, the arms will come up against the back of the lining, tightening the hook permanently into the wall (see photograph).

Unfortunately, should you need to remove this hook, the toggle will be lost but, as they only cost a few cents, who cares?

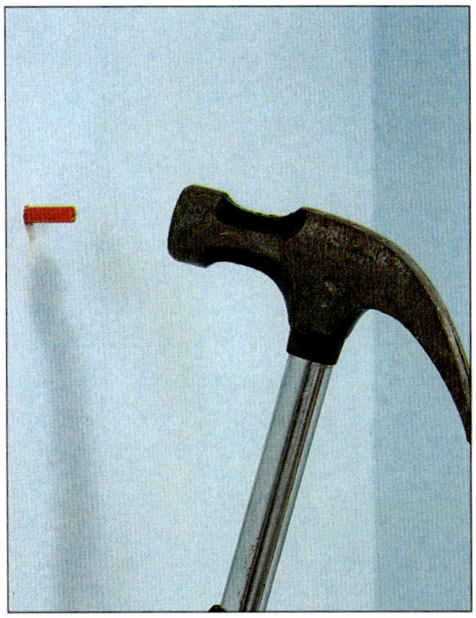

Hammer the plastic plug into the pre-drilled hole.

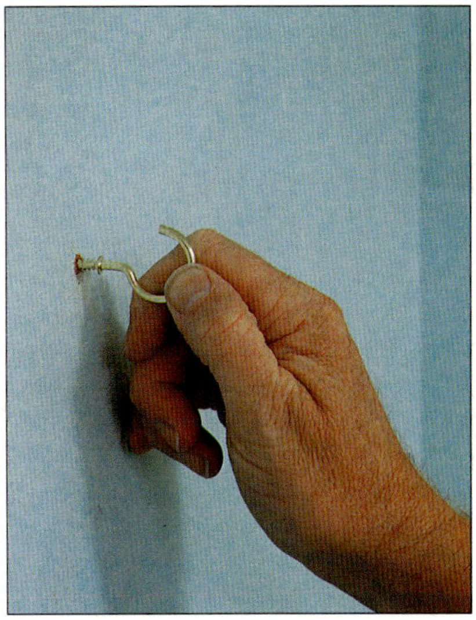

Screw the hook into the plug until the shoulder bites.

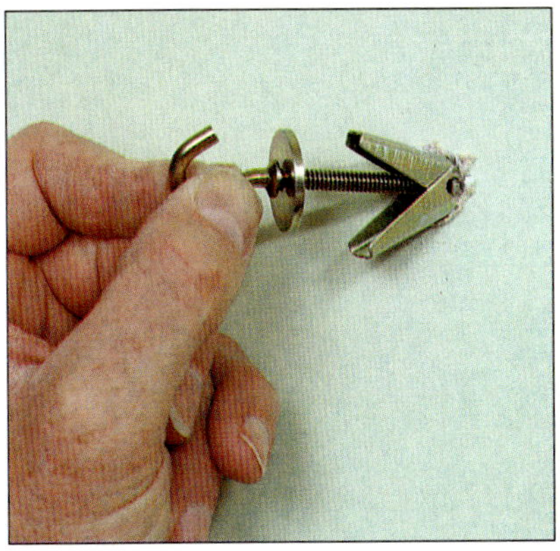

The toggle will fold flat as it goes through the hole.

The finished job is very strong.

The picture rehung.

Rectifying Lifting or Bubbling Laminate

Plastic laminates, properly glued, provide a serviceable and attractive finish for surfaces like kitchen and bathroom bench tops and doors. They excel where there is moisture.

The surface, providing it is not cut or subjected to high temperature, is virtually indestructible. However, because of moisture or faulty manufacture, problems can arise from poor adherence of the material to the backing. The result is that the bench top can bubble or an edge strip can lift. If it's within the warranty period then make some appropriate noises! If not, you will probably be able to fix it quite easily yourself. Here's what to do.

Plastic laminate kitchen benchtops

For a bubble, use a hot iron to warm the whole area.

Laminate Bubbles

Fixing the bubble problem may be easy. The only equipment you will require is an iron or hairdryer plus a hammer and block, assuming that a rubber-based contact glue has been used (see Glues).

FIRST PROCEDURE

1 Using a hairdryer on the highest temperature or an iron set where it's almost too hot to touch (325°F), warm the whole area for at least five minutes. This will soften the glue and make it active again.

2 Using the hammer and block, tap the bubble down. If you are lucky, it will adhere once again and the problem is fixed.

But if it doesn't . . .

The reason could be that a PVC glue (which can't be re-activated) has been applied or there is insufficient contact glue in the offending area. In either case you will have to drill one or two holes in the bubble so you can inject enough contact or PVC glue into the space to cover both surfaces.

TOOLS AND MATERIALS

You will need a hand drill, a 2–3 mm drill bit, a heavy weight, a hammer, smooth block and contact or PVC glue.

SECOND PROCEDURE

1 After drilling the hole or holes (say one every 50 mm of bubble), check which type of glue has been used. You will find that contact glue is a thick yellowy-brown colour whereas the PVC is almost clear. Purchase a small quantity of a similar glue.

2 Pour or rub a liberal quantity of the glue into the holes and press the bubble flat to help spread the glue out.

If using PVC, immediately apply a heavy weight to the spot for at least 12 hours. Watch you don't stick the weight to the bench! Some plastic wrap will ensure this doesn't happen.

If using rubber contact, leave the two surfaces apart for approximately 15 minutes (until touch dry) and then tap the bubble down with your hammer and a smooth block. Apply some weight for a few hours just to make sure.

3 Depending on the colour and pattern of the surface, fill each hole with a spot of epoxy glue and touch it up with matching paint. Alternatively, keep your breadboard or an ornament on top of the holes.

Lifting Laminate

Laminate which peels or lifts off can also be restuck provided you use a glue similar to the original. But remember, to be successful both the underside of the laminate and the backing surface must be completely dry and free from all grease, oil, food matter, etc.

PROCEDURE

1 Wedge the gap open as far as possible (but watch you don't crack the laminate!) with a paddlepop stick, screwdriver or knife. Scrape out all foreign material until surfaces are spotlessly clean (some sandpapering could help), then leave it wedged open for a minimum of 48 hours to help it to dry. If the subsurface is saturated, a hairdryer set on high and blown into the area will hasten the drying.

2 Apply the correct glue and fix following the procedure above.

If you strike any further problems contact your laminate or glue supplier. The manufacturers have printed information on their products which they are only too happy to send to you. They also employ technical people who are eagerly waiting to answer all your tricky questions. The manufacturers want to see you, the customer, happy with their products.

For lifting laminate, clean out the gap with a screwdriver.

You can use a hairdryer to speed up the drying process.

Apply glue with spreader and leave till touch dry.

Make sure contact glue is touch dry before joining surfaces.

Tap the laminate down with a hammer and a smooth block.

Fixing a Damp Patch on a Wall

Flaking or peeling paint, crazing or mildewed plaster, or timber decay that begins well above the floor line (assuming it's not caused by rising damp, a broken roof tile, faulty roof flashings or a leaking valley gutter) suggest two things:

- If it's under or adjacent to a window or external door, the window flashings are either not working or are non-existent;
- If it's elsewhere, there may be an obstruction in the wall cavity (if there is one) which is bridging water across from the outside.

Window and Door Flashings

In cavity brick, brick veneer and timber frame construction, all windows and external doors should have head flashings over the top of them. All windows and some doors have sill flashing as well (see Diagram 1). A flashing is a thin, waterproof material such as lead, aluminium or plastic, which is placed in a position vulnerable to weather to stop external water penetration.

Unfortunately, in the hands of poor builders, it is the kind of item that is sometimes forgotten altogether or, all too often, installed incorrectly.

If there are no flashings, other than trying to waterproof the exterior wall by using a waterproofing paint or clear silicone sealer, and using silicone caulking to try to seal off any gaps, the only proper way to fix the problem is to get a builder to take off the internal frame trims, cut the fixings with a hacksaw, completely remove the frame, and then reflash the opening properly.

If the flashings are in place but damaged, taking off the internal trims and using liberal amounts of silicone in the suspect places may effect a cure. If it doesn't, taking the frame out is the most foolproof solution, but well beyond the capability of the average do-it-yourselfer.

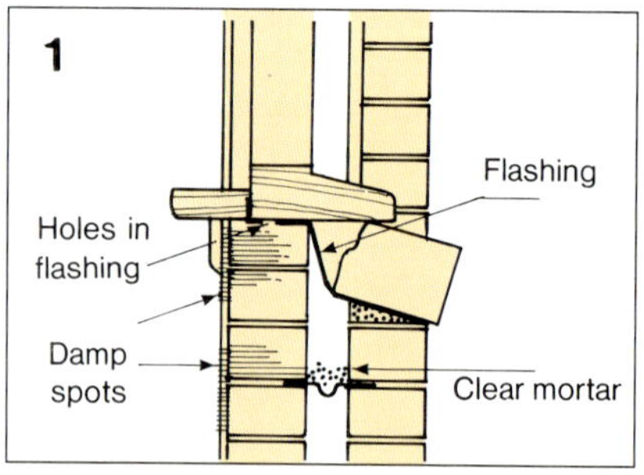

Section showing flashing under sill

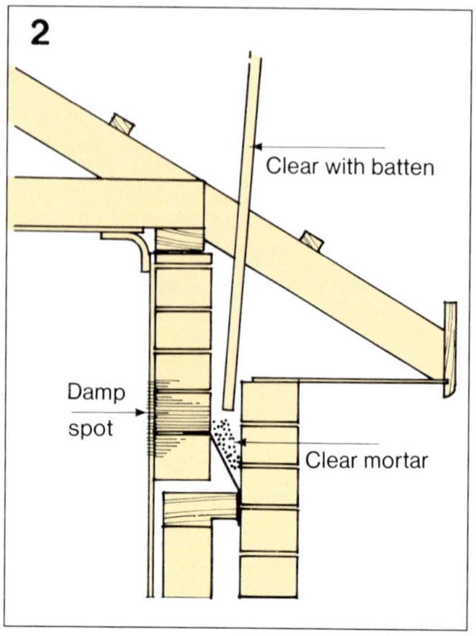

Section showing dampness caused by mortar droppings in a cavity wall

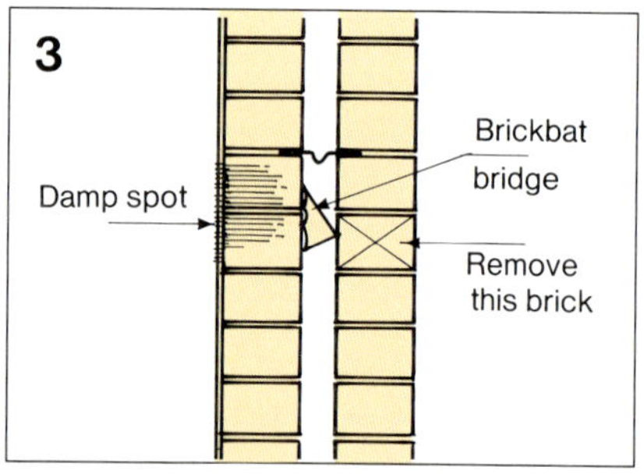

Brickbat jammed in cavity wall

Clearing Cavity Bridges

Bridges across cavities in double brick or brick veneer construction are caused either by:

- a brickbat that is jammed in the cavity and left there by a careless builder or bricklayer; or
- mortar droppings that are caught on the wall ties; or
- mortar droppings that are lying on the top of the head flashing.

PROCEDURE

1 To establish the reason, get up on the roof (see Repairing a Leaking Roof) with a torch and lift a few tiles directly over the trouble spot. This should enable you to look down the cavity to see what the problem is.

2 In the case of the last two causes, a long batten poked down the cavity should dislodge the bridge (see Diagram 2). Over a window, watch you don't poke a hole through the flashing itself.

3 A tightly jammed brickbat is a more serious problem. First, try to dislodge it with the batten. If it's stuck, correctly establish where it is (the batten will help), then, with a plugging chisel and lump hammer, from the outside, chop out the brick joints around the brick opposite the obstruction (see Diagram 3). Remove the brick, then the bat, and relay the brick (see Relaying Loose Bricks).

Solid Brick Walls

One solution is to render the outside of the wall to increase its impermeability. This shouldn't be done if the wall has been painted with a sealer because the render may not adhere properly. Although a 1 part of cement to 3 parts of sand mix is strong and fairly waterproof, it is more likely to crack and can in fact lock moisture behind it. This moisture, unable to get away through the outside wall, will (you guessed it!) gravitate inwards.

Use a 1 of cement, 1 of lime, 6 of sand mix and consider using a stucco finish because not only is it less likely to crack, but the surface area is increased, thereby improving evaporation.

If you've tried painting the outside of the porous brick with a sealer or waterproofing paint and you've had no success, then there is another solution. It's called battening out.

What you do is to batten the inside of the wall and apply a separate internal lining. This then creates a cavity which leaves the damp wall to its own devices. The size of the battens and the space between them will depend on the lining you're using. A waterproof barrier should be inserted between each batten and the wall.

The plugs and battens should be of a timber species that won't rot. Western red cedar or a durable hardwood would be suitable. The fastenings should be brass or hotdip galvanised.

Painting the back of the lining sheets with an oil-based paint before fixing will help to seal them off from any dampness. Put a few air vents in the lining to ensure some air circulation behind the lining.

Repainting

Once the problem is solved, the wall should be left until the moisture has dried out. It will require approximately four months for a brick wall to dry out fully but that time can be accelerated by use of artificial heating (hairdryers or radiators). While the wall is drying, the faulty paint should be removed (this will increase the wall's exposure to air and heat). If the paint is oil-based and the rendered area is large it may pay to use a heat gun or blowlamp to thoroughly burn the paint. Then simply scrape it off.

Alternatively, using some rough sandpaper, a cork block and a plentiful supply of elbow grease, sand the patch back to bare plaster.

To lessen the possibility of the patch showing in the finished paintwork, thin the perimeter edges with fine sandpaper on a block so there is no discernible ridge. This is called feathering.

When the patch is fully dry, check that the surface has no whitish deposit on it. If it has, then efflorescence has taken place. This means that soluble salts from within the brick or render have been brought to the surface by the evaporating water. Paint the patch with a 5% solution of muriatic acid and rinse well. Redry the patch before painting.

If using oil-based paint you must apply a suitable sealer, then an undercoat, and finish with one or two layers of a finish coat. With water-based paints (acrylics and plastic) the procedure is greatly simplified. Some can be painted straight on while others only require the first coat to be slightly thinned.

Peeling paint is an indication of dampness in the wall.

Remove the faulty paint with a scraper.

Sand the surface and edges with sandpaper and a cork block.

When the patch is completely dry repaint the wall.

Foundation-based Water Damage

Water is essential for human life. However, if it finds its way into the wrong place in a home it can cause untold damage. A lot of potential water damage in your home can emanate from the ground.

The ground can be likened to a piece of blotting paper. It absorbs moisture in wet conditions and dries out in droughts. Many of the commonly used building materials are porous and also absorb moisture. Therefore, it is essential to stop the moisture movement by providing a barrier.

In brickwork, this barrier is created by building a waterproof membrane such as plastic or aluminium strip into the brick joint during construction. This barrier is called a damp proof course (DPC).

If the DPC is left out or damaged by uncaring or unsupervised bricklayers, water will soak up the wall and, if it is an internal wall, cause the paint to peel off, mildew to flourish, etc.

Unfortunately, the only way to rectify the problem is to replace the barrier. This involves chopping out the joint and inserting an appropriate DPC. It is a time-consuming and heart-breaking job, one that, unless the area is very small, should be done by an expert.

Water Diversion

Another way to lessen potential water damage is to stop it reaching the property. This can be achieved by building retaining walls (which should be designed by an engineer) putting in properly constructed agricultural drains (information on which can be obtained from the CSIRO via their building science notes), sloping the soil or footpaths away from external walls, etc.

Increasing Ventilation

Other common dampness problems, even if the DPC is satisfactory and water is completely diverted, are caused by:

- underground seepage,
- a severe plumbing or drainage leak (which can easily be detected and rectified), or
- insufficient ventilation under a house as a result of having too few vents or because they've been blocked by built-up gardens, paths or even shrubs.

The result of this moisture in the long term is that the under-floor timbers will rot. Short-term indications are cupping of flooring or even swelling that lifts the boards up off the joists.

Periodic six-monthly inspection under a house will ensure that all is well. If rotting (which is caused by fungi that feed on the timber) is discovered, then clearing or dramatically increasing the number of vents will help. For indivertible seepage, laying a cover of plastic membrane over the complete area (making sure you tape the joints) will seal much of the moisture off.

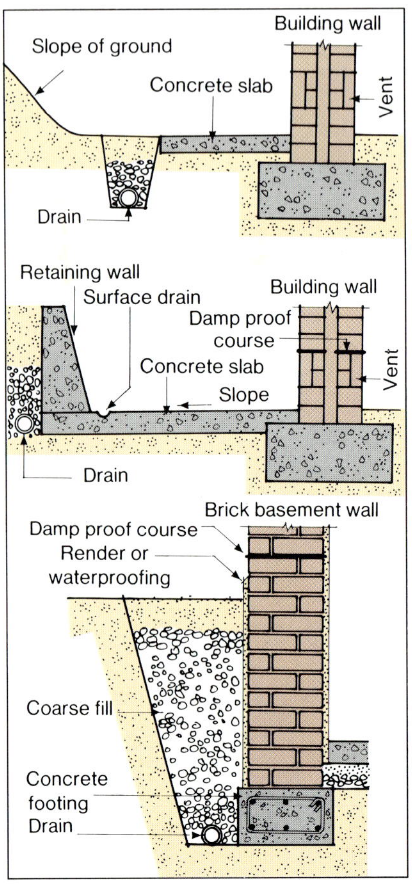

Waterproofing an Existing Wall

Waterproofing can be achieved by painting a wall with a waterproof paint or, if earth fill is pressing against it, by completely removing the fill and following one of the procedures below.

PROCEDURE

1 Waterproofers Made from bitumen, latex rubber, water-based epoxies and silicones, these products are painted onto the wall to provide an impermeable barrier to water. Thus a back-filled internal wall can be painted on the inside or an exposed external wall can be sealed on the outside (the latter being the more effective). The efficacy of the product will depend amongst other things on the severity and pressure of the water penetration; how dirty, wet, mouldy, flaking, crumbly or efflorescent the wall is; and whether the wall is exposed to the sun or not.

2 Waterproofing retaining walls Walls become retaining walls when buildings are excavated into the ground or where land is terraced. They must be properly designed and built to avoid overturning and leaking. If an existing wall is leaking and diversion of the water is impossible then the best solution is firstly to dig out the old fill. Cut it clear of the bottom of the wall by 600 mm and slope it back at an angle of approximately 45°. Apply a waterproofer or, if the flow is considerable, you can stick bitumen-impregnated felt to the wall with bitumen paint.

Then lay a large seepage drain along the wall. Make sure the bottom of the pipe is level with the bottom of the footing. Run it away from the house to a suitable pit or to the street. Then fill the space with a porous backfill such as gravel or crushed stone and cover with a path that slopes *away* from the house.

Replacing a Few Ceramic Tiles

Replacing a few loose tiles is not very difficult. By following the simple step-by-step procedure which follows you can do it yourself and achieve a professional finish as well.

Remember that most tile suppliers love do-it-yourselfers of either sex and will supply you with all materials and lots of free advice. They often hire tools as well.

To the job! Lightly tap the area surrounding the offending tiles and listen to see if the rest of the tiles are sound. If so, breathe a sigh of relief. If they're all drummy (a hollow, echoing noise) call in a tiler. To retile a complete bathroom is too big a job unless you're especially clever and have lots of time.

Next establish the reason for the looseness. It will usually be:

- a water leak in the wall plumbing (you must get a plumber to fix this problem before it causes more damage than just loose tiles);
- the wrong adhesive was used, the adhesive was poorly applied, or the previous surface preparation was faulty.

In some cases it may also be that the grouting (the coloured material in the tile joints) is failing and letting in water. In this situation once you have retiled and grouted the loose area, paint the other joints with a silicone sealer or, if you want a top quality job, rake the joints out and regrout them (see Regrouting a Shower Recess).

Sand off old adhesive from the backs of the tiles.

The completed job with the loose tiles back in place.

Spread the adhesive on the backs of the tiles.

Mix the grout to a paste and rub into the joints.

TOOLS AND MATERIALS

You'll need a putty knife for scraping, a sponge and a notched spreader (which often comes with the adhesive).

Go to the tile shop, describe the situation, and ask for a suitable adhesive, some tile spacers (unless the tiles have spacer lugs on their edges) and a coloured grout to match the existing.

PROCEDURE

For total success, the back of the tiles and the wall must be clean, dry, firm and flat.

1 If a tap is in the way, unscrew it and then remove the loose tiles. Scrape or sand off any lumps of old adhesive and clean each surface with a strong detergent (which must be rinsed off).

2 In the case of new, unpainted gypsum board, it must be sealed by painting the area to be tiled with a multi-purpose primer or a polyurethane paint.

If the surface has been painted, scrape off any flaking paint and roughen the old surface with sandpaper. Never use paint stripper, because it leaves a chemical residue which could weaken the adhesive. In all cases, if the surface is uneven, plaster it smooth with a compatible filler.

3 Spread the adhesive evenly over the area to be tiled (2–3 mm thick). In hard-to-reach areas apply a double thickness to the back of each tile.

4 Press the tiles into position working from the bottom up. Push the spacers into place as you go to maintain an even joint. For large areas periodically check that the new tiles line up with the existing ones by using a straight piece of timber or a level. Wipe off any excess adhesive with a sponge and allow the tiles to dry.

5 Mix the grout to a paste and rub into the joints, making sure you clean off the excess *before* it dries. After it sets, polish the tiles with a dry cloth.

Loose Jambs in Brickwork

Fixing a wobbly jamb in an external or internal brick wall looks a daunting task. Loose jambs in a timber frame wall can simply be renailed, but how do you fix into bricks?

The answer is simple: use masonry bolts. You just bore a hole through the jamb and into the brickwork with a masonry drill, insert the masonry bolt, then tighten the nut. The bolt locks itself into the brick by expanding the plastic or metal sleeve that is part of it. Once tightened, the bolt provides secure anchorage and stabilises the jamb.

Secure the jamb in place with a temporary block.

Bore a hole in the jamb with a speed drill.

TOOLS AND MATERIALS

Electric drill, masonry drill bit to suit the diameter and length of the masonry bolt, spanner, tape and pencil, a speed drill bit 10 mm larger than the bolt head (but only if you want the head of the bolt sunk below the face of the jamb), and an old sheet to collect the mess will be needed.

You will also need one masonry bolt for each 450 mm of loose jamb. The length of the bolt must be sufficient to go through the thickness of the jamb and project at least 50 mm into the brickwork. The diameter required depends on the length but will typically be 6 mm.

PROCEDURE

1 Place the jamb in its original position. This can be found by looking on the floor at the old paint line. Secure the jamb with some temporary blocks tacked to both floor and jamb. Use fine gauge nails to avoid damage.

2 If you want the bolt head to finish *below* the face of the jamb (it looks better), use your speed drill to bore a hole into the jamb face or rebate 20 mm deep wherever you have decided to place a bolt (the first one should be around 180 mm from the floor). Avoid brick joints.

Remember, if it's an external brick wall, there is usually a cavity between the two layers of brickwork. A brick is 110 mm wide and render is usually 10 mm thick, so you should be able to position the bolt so it's at least 40 mm away from the edge of the brick. For narrow jambs this could mean that you have to put the bolts in the jamb rebate.

3 Next place the masonry bit in the electric drill and bore through the sunk holes until you hit brickwork. Stop and mark the drill with a pencil line and withdraw it. Mark another location 50 mm higher up the drill and wrap masking tape round this mark. Go on drilling until the timber touches the tape. Complete all the holes similarly.

4 Insert the bolts and, with your spanner or pliers, tighten the nut or bolt head.

5 Check that the door closes. If the jamb has gone in too far, take off the architrave, loosen the bolts, lever the jamb back out to its correct position with a chisel, then pack in behind the jamb with bits of ply or fibre cement. Retighten the bolts and replace the architrave.

If you have sunk the bolt heads in, you could fill the large holes with a suitable filler or, better still, glue in a piece of wooden dowel of the same diameter.

If you haven't, cut off the excess thread with a hacksaw, and paint the protruding fastenings the same colour as the jamb.

Drill a hole in the brickwork with a masonry drill.

Tighten the nut with pliers until it is firm.

Fill the hole in the jamb with a piece of wooden dowel.

Repairing a Rotting Gate

Gates, because of their exposure to the weather, often rot. This destructive decay of timber is caused by fungi, a minute form of plant life. The spores from rotting wood float through the air and can alight on exposed timber. If the timber is damp the spores germinate and spread, eating the timber away, leaving only a crumbling mass.

The way to avoid rotting is to install a gate made from either a decay resistant timber or a timber that has been treated with a preservative. However, if an existing gate is beginning to decay you must quickly remove the rotting pieces and replace them with a more durable timber.

Of the Australian timbers that have a natural resistance to decay, cypress pine is one of the best. Western red cedar, imported from Canada, though soft, is very resistant to decay and is therefore suitable for exterior use.

An alternative is to use treated radiata pine, which is easily recognised by its greenish tinge. This cheap, fast-growing timber is impregnated with a poisonous chemical that kills fungi and termites, thus preserving the otherwise susceptible wood.

Remove the rotting parts of the gate with a claw hammer.

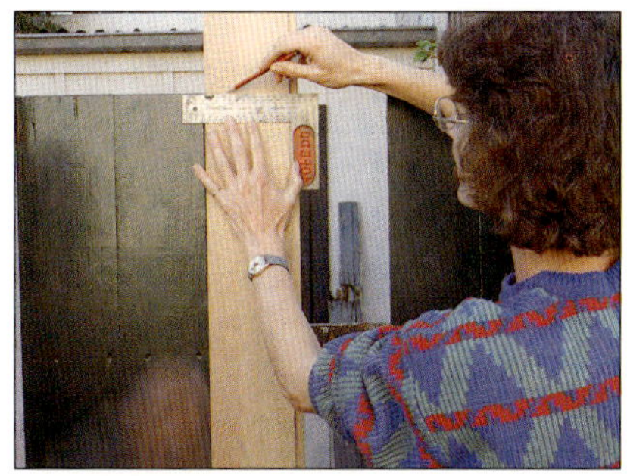

Carefully mark the new pieces to the correct length.

You can fix the new pieces in place using screws.

Alternatively use nails and fix the nails by clenching.

TOOLS AND MATERIALS

A screwdriver, hammer and nail punch, a square, a panel or hand saw, tape and pencil and perhaps a hacksaw. You'll need timber of a similar length and section size to the pieces to be replaced. Ideally, fastenings should be brass. Ferrous fastenings must be galvanised.

PROCEDURE

1 Using the screwdriver, take the gate off its hinges. Alternatively the gate can be repaired in position. If the screws have badly rusted you may need to cut them off with a hacksaw. If the hinges are rusty, remove them and either buy new galvanised ones or, if they're in fair condition, wire brush them back to bare metal and paint them with a cold-galvanising paint.

2 A typical gate has its members butted together and is held together with nails, screws or bolts. Assuming it's not a framed gate and has no interlocking joints like the mortice and tenon, it should be possible to remove the pieces that are rotting with the claw on the hammer or by undoing the bolts or screws. Make sure you remove every rotting piece, otherwise the rot could flare up again.

3 Carefully mark the new pieces to the correct length and shape and, laying them on a low wall or bench, cut them to size with your hand or panel saw. Use a coping saw and fine rasp to cut and finish curved shapes.

When cutting the boards, mark a fine line across the face and down both edges. Place the saw on the *waste* side of the line with the edge of the teeth just touching the line. When you're finished sawing the lines should still be visible.

4 Lay the gate on top of some scrap blocks on a solid surface (such as a concrete slab or deck) and, using nails, screws, etc., fix the pieces in place.

To increase the holding power of nails use ones which have flat heads and are 10 mm longer than the total thickness of the gate. When the pieces are well nailed, turn the gate over and bend the projecting nails over in the direction of the wood grain. This is called clenching. Punch the ends below the surface. This will ensure they never pull out.

5 Prop the gate into position using blocks and then rescrew the hinges into place.

6 If the original gate is unpainted and made with a rot-prone timber, either cover the rest of it with some fungus-inhibiting preservative or paint the whole gate with a water-soluble paint. It could help to clear away some of the shrubbery which may be contributing to the humid environment.

Repainting a Room

Repainting a few rooms can be fun and it lends a fresh, long-lasting lease of life to your home. It's easy providing you follow some simple steps.

Surface Preparation

This is always tedious but it's essential for good results. Remember paint will not adhere properly to a surface that is incorrectly prepared.

New work Metal: remove all rust, dirt and oil.

Wood: sand smooth, cover resinous knots with knotting, and fill all small holes with putty.

Gypsum plaster: make sure it's clean and thoroughly dry. Brush or vacuum the wall to remove all jointing cement dust. Fill holes with cellulose filler.

Bricks, concrete and plaster: leave to dry for 12 weeks if using oil-based paints. If using water-based paint, clean thoroughly.

Old work Strip off flaking, crazing or bubbling paint using a blowtorch or heat gun and scraper, but not on fibrous or gypsum plaster for obvious reasons. Alternatively use a chemical stripper (wear rubber gloves and make sure the room is well ventilated). Small areas can be scraped clean, sanded or wire-brushed. Fill all cracks, dents and chips with a cellulose filler or putty and sand smooth. Remove any mould or efflorescence (a white, salt deposit that leaches out of damp bricks).

Some wallpapers, if sound, may be painted over (but a sealer may be required). Check with the wallpaper supplier or manufacturer if known or try a small area first to see if the colours leach out or the wallpaper glue is affected. If any doubt exists, strip it off with a wallpaper steamer which you can hire. Alternatively, soak it off with warm water.

If paintwork is sound just make sure you clean off any grease spots, stains, etc., with detergent or sugar soap, and rinse clean. Sand lightly to increase adhesion.

With nail pops in gypsum plaster, punch the nails heads further in and fill the hole with cornice cement. Then, when dry, skim over it with a generous layer of jointing cement applied with a broad knife. Sand with fine adhesive paper.

HANDY PAINTING HINTS

- Check that paint is sound by sticking some cellulose tape onto the surface in several places. If paint adheres to it when you pull it off, the surface should be stripped.
- If you're in the middle of painting and lunch intervenes, or you want to stop for a cup of tea, simply wrap the roller or brush in a plastic wrap or a plastic bag to seal it from the air — it will keep it from drying out for an hour or so.
- Rollers should be hung up to dry otherwise you'll get a flat spot in the nap.
- Brushes will also retain their shape better if after you've cleaned them thoroughly (paying particular attention to the area near the handle), you shape the wet bristles to a proper brush shape.

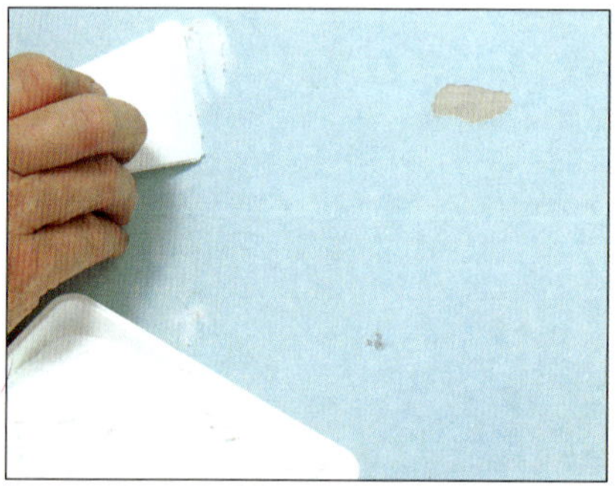

Fill holes in gypsum plaster with cellulose filler.

Sand painted wood lightly to increase adhesion.

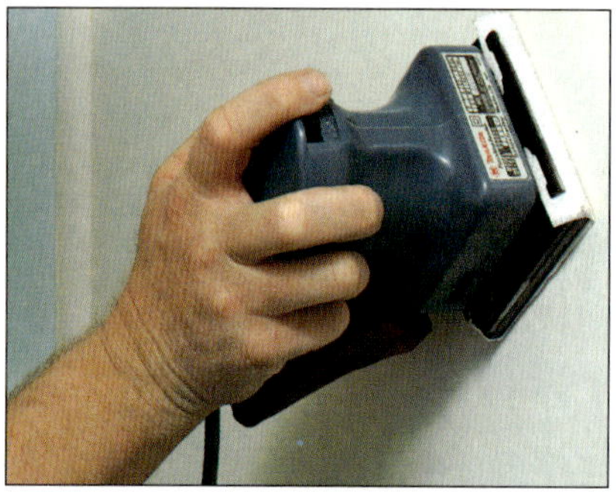

An orbital sander makes the job easier.

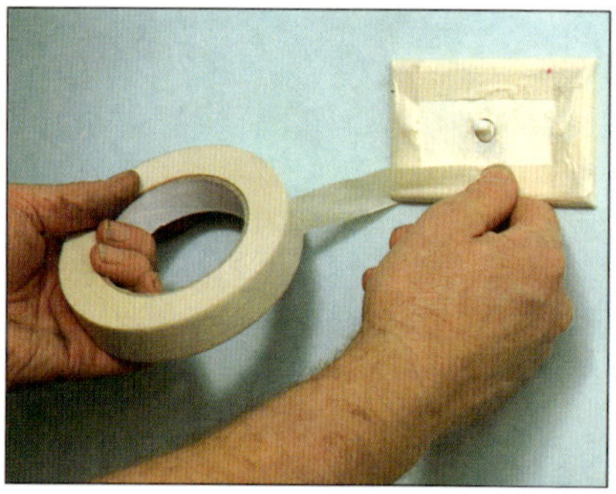

Masking tape round light switches facilitates cutting in.

If the old paint is sound, washing may be the only preparation needed.

Use a roller to paint the ceiling, working towards the light source.

Use a brush for cornices and cutting in.

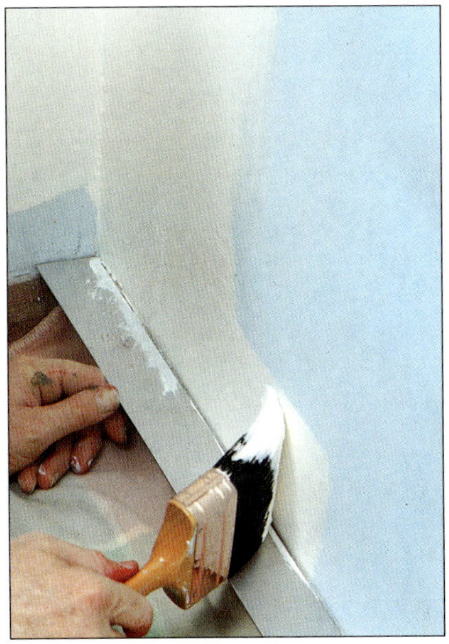

A strip of thin metal is useful when cutting in.

Use the narrow brush for cutting in round windows and architraves.

TOOLS AND MATERIALS

Use a brush for all wood priming and detail work. A good quality 50 mm and a 100 mm cover most jobs.

Rollers with a tray are especially quick for walls, ceilings and flush doors and give a good, slightly textured finish. Rollers (made from foam, lambswool or mohair — different ones suit different paints) and brushes should be well cleaned and dried after each use in the appropriate cleaner to ensure long life.

A plentiful supply of old rags and sponges should be on hand to wipe up spills and drops. A handy item is a 600 × 100 mm strip of thin metal or plastic. This strip can be pressed against skirtings, etc., so that cutting in is easier and faster. Paint quantities are shown in the chart below.

PROCEDURE

1 Begin with the ceilings, then the walls, and finish with the windows, doors and trims. Empty the room as much as possible and cover the remaining furniture (pushed into the centre of the room) and carpets with old sheets, etc. Masking tape around power points and switches facilitates cutting in, but don't leave it for too long in case it sticks permanently! Make sure there is plenty of natural or artificial light to reduce the likelihood of missed or thin spots.

2 **Ceilings** A plank laid across two stools or strong wooden boxes makes a convenient scaffold. Alternatively use a step ladder. Stir the paint well and fill the tray halfway up the slope. Work the roller into the paint until it's covered and then roll it evenly against the textured tray surface to stop dripping. Apply working from the corners out. Roll out any overlaps. Keep a brush on the tray for painting cornices, getting into corners and finishing against trims. Move towards your light source in 800 mm strips.

3 **Walls** Follow the same procedure as for ceilings except that you begin in a corner and work from the ceiling down. Paint a thin strip with your brush along the cornice and skirting first and then fill in between with the roller.

4 **Doors, windows and skirting** Do the trims (architraves) first, then the frames, then the sashes or doors. Flush doors can be done with the roller providing you take off the door handles. Moulded doors, architraves, and window frames and sashes require a brush. Doors should be finished on the edges first, then the faces. Paint around handles first (though it is better to remove them), and then finish the rest.

Again stir the paint well, dip the brush in, remove excess paint by stroking once against the side of the tin, and then, using 300 mm strokes running parallel with the wood grain, apply evenly. Too much paint will cause runs and too little will expose the undercoat, primer or previous finish. Brush out overlaps. When using enamel, finish as you go because it dries quickly, especially on a hot day. Don't attempt to go back over a sticky area!

For cutting in against walls use a thin strip of metal or plastic but watch that you keep wiping the edge clean or the paint will run in underneath.

If you experience any difficulties ring or write to the paint manufacturers. They employ experts who are paid to assist with technical advice or send printed information. But first, read the directions on the tin carefully. It will save you much embarrassment!

Repairing Timber Floors

Before new floor coverings are put down, old coverings have to be removed and the floor carefully prepared. Any marked unevenness will clearly show through linoleum, sheet vinyl or vinyl tiles. Carpet will wear unevenly if the surface is irregular. It is therefore necessary to make the floor smooth and even by filling any holes in the boards, removing nails that stick up plus any bits of the old covering material, and then sanding.

First step is to lift and remove the old covering. A pinch bar is a useful tool for levering up carpet and sheet vinyl, although the claw on a hammer will also do the job. Use the wedge-shaped end to lever it up, and then the curved end for removing the fastenings. If the head of the nail should snap off then simply drive it in level with the floor. If you don't have a pinch bar, a pair of pincers could be used to remove headless nails or staples. For lifting vinyl or cork tiles, a spade is useful.

After the covering has been lifted and removed, examine the exposed flooring carefully. If it is badly split in many places, or the boards have shrunk excessively leaving gaps everywhere, or there are countless holes, it would be better to cover the whole floor with a layer of tempered hardboard or fibrous cement rather than to attempt to fix it (see Laying Cork or Vinyl Tiles).

If it's in fair condition, punch the heads of all protruding flooring nails below the surface of the floor about 2 mm. Use a nail punch that has a tip the same diameter as the nail head. Using a finer one will only damage the tip, while a larger one will make too large a hole. Be careful of your fingers! Make sure the face of the hammer is clean by lightly sanding it. This will prevent it slipping off the punch.

Once all the nails are punched the next step is to fill the holes. Small holes can be filled with a hard-drying, non-shrinking cellulose filler. Your hardware store will advise you which is the best type. Mix carefully and slightly over-fill the hole. Sand off flush when completely dry. If the filling compound keeps dropping right through the hole it may be necessary to get under the floor and nail a scrap piece of fibro or tin over the hole until the filler dries. Watch out for spiders!

Large Holes

Large holes or missing boards may need to be filled with a piece of similar flooring or timber. Cut the offending piece 10 mm clear of the joist at either end with the tip of a tenon saw (alternatively, bore a hole and use a fine keyhole saw) and lever it out. In the case of tongue and groove boards you will also need to use the tenon saw to rip off the tenon.

Nail a scrap piece of hardwood batten on the sides of the joist to give support to the new piece. Make it level with the underneath of the flooring to provide support. Then neatly cut in and fit the new piece, again ripping off the tenon. Nail it in and punch the nails.

A light sanding of the floor with a cork block and garnet paper or, better still, a belt sander, will remove all minor irregularities and any substances which may interfere with the adhesive bond.

The preparation is now complete and should ensure your new carpet or vinyl looks perfect when it's laid.

The first stop is to lift and remove the old floor covering.

Lift the smooth edge, if any, with a pinch bar.

Extract protruding nails with a pinch bar.

You may find a hole like this in your floor.

Fill the hole with a scrap piece of timber.

Clearing a Blocked Sink

I'll bet you looked disbelievingly at a sink full of lukewarm, greasy water and then you reached for this book muttering, 'Help!' For weeks the sink has taken longer and longer to empty and now, just when visitors are coming, it's finally stopped. Typical, eh?

There are three ways to attack the problem: using chemicals; using a rubber plunger or sink pump; or unscrewing the S-bend under the sink (assuming it doesn't have a cleaning eye).

Chemicals

There are on the market proprietary products designed to be put down the drainage system to eat away some of the things which may be blocking the line. Read the instructions carefully before you use the product. Chemicals are usually dangerous.

Their success varies depending on their quality, the type of chemical used, what is causing the problem, how early you attack it and, most importantly, how long you can afford to wait, assuming the sink is blocked. Often the chemicals must be left overnight.

For a quicker reaction in your sink you may have to buy or borrow a plunger (or a sink pump).

Plunger

The idea of a plunger, which is like a huge suction cup, is to create a pressure which may dislodge the object that is blocking your sink. By placing the plunger over the waste hole and vigorously pumping it up and down you create a force which, if you're lucky and the blockage is minor, may send the tea leaves or food matter on their way. The more efficient and more expensive sink pump gives greater pressure.

If, however, after much effort, the plunger doesn't work, then your last course of action is to disconnect the S-bend under the sink and manually clear the blockage.

The S-bend is a remarkably simple but effective way of sealing off bad odours which might come back up the plumbing pipes.

Removing the S-Bend

TOOLS

You'll need a bucket or basin to catch the sink water. If the large plastic nuts are too tight to move by hand you may also need to borrow a large pair of multigrips or wrench.

PROCEDURE

1 Clear the items from around the under-sink plumbing.

2 Place the bucket or basin in position.

3 Begin to unscrew the nuts on either side of the bend. (If it's an old metal type there may be a small eye on the bottom of the bend which can be unscrewed with a spanner. The blockage can then be cleared with a small piece of wire or a bottle brush).

4 Remove the bend, clean out the blockage, then screw it tightly back in place. Most plastic fittings are self-sealing. Metal sometimes needs to be caulked with Vaseline or thread tape.

5 Run some water and check the joints for leaks while saying a few prayers. If the water flows away quickly you've solved the problem. Clever you!

If it doesn't, then there is obviously a blockage further down the line which could be caused by such ominous things as tree roots, a blocked grease trap, etc. Ring your favourite plumber and leave a 'Help!' message on the answering phone.

Unscrew the nuts on either side of the S-bend under the sink.

Remove the bend.

Clean out the bend with a flexible brush.

After replacing the bend run some water and check for leaks.

Repairing and Leaf-proofing Gutters

Major problems with gutters, besides rusting, are that the brackets come loose, they hold water, or they leak at the joints.

Leaks

Check all joints in the gutter. For leaking ones, spread the joint, clean the overlapping metal surfaces thoroughly and dry them. Then, using a flexible silicone caulking compound, reseal the joints.

Leaves

Leaves hold moisture, increasing the risk of rusting. They can also eventually block the downpipes, which will cause the gutters to overflow. This could lead to damage to gardens or the risk of dampness in external walls. You can clean them out from a ladder or from the roof surface. Use a putty knife and bucket (the mulch is good for the garden). If there is an excessive number of leaves you would be well advised to purchase an anti-leaf system from your hardware store (see photographs) and install it in accordance with the manufacturer's instructions. These products are specially designed to fit over the top of the gutter to stop any leaves entering it. There are a number of types at varying prices. As with everything, relate the rapidly escalating cost to the often marginal benefit!

Use a flexible silicone caulking compound to seal leaking joints.

Fixing Loose Brackets

Loose brackets usually occur because the nails in the gutter brackets have rusted through or the fascia has rotted or split and the nails have nothing solid to grip into. If the gutter is loose it may no longer fall correctly to the downpipes, meaning water lies in the bottom. This will eventually cause a ferrous metal gutter to rust out. Also if it's loose, it could come adrift in a high wind or heavy rain.

PROCEDURE

1 If the gutter is not too high, borrow or hire a ladder and get up to see what the cause is. Remember that ladders are potentially dangerous if they are not set up properly (see Repairing a Leaking Roof).

2 With a pair of pliers or multigrips, undo the front of the brackets where they clip over the edge of the gutter for the full length of the run. To do this you will have to move the ladder several times unless you have a good head for heights and the roof is not too steep. In that case, wearing sandshoes and walking on the front edges of the tiles, you can walk along the roof and unclip the brackets.

3 With a long piece of timber push the gutter up off the brackets where it's loose and prop it up. Alternatively, lift it out of the brackets while you sit on the roof and lay it on the tiles.

4 Move the loose brackets along a bit and renail them into solid timber with galvanised clouts. Make sure you nail them back at the same height as they were (a level is handy for this). If the fascia is rotten or badly cracked along its length, you will need to call in a carpenter to replace part or all of it and then a plumber to refix the gutter with the correct fall.

5 Replace the gutter and carefully bend each clip back over the nose of the gutter.

With a pair of pliers, undo the front of the brackets.

Remove the loose brackets from the fascia board.

Move the loose bracket along and renail it into solid timber.

Install a leaf-proofing system to keep leaves out of your gutter.

Fixing Sticking Drawers

Are you having problems with your drawers? Sticking or coming-apart drawers create an unwanted eddy in the flow of household affairs. Fixing them is easy if you have a few minutes to spare.

First you have to identify the problem.

Why Drawers Stick

There are six typical reasons why drawers stick.

1. The drawers may have been accidentally put in the wrong place. If they're the same size, try rearranging the order to see if that helps.

2. Dampness, caused by such things as a plumbing leak, rising damp, or prolonged humidity, may be swelling the timber or particle board members. Check the under-sink plumbing if the drawer is in a kitchen or bathroom and rectify if necessary. For other rooms, move the chest of drawers or dresser out from the wall and feel the wall surface. If it is very damp or mildewed check the under-house drainage. If everything seems to be in order, call in an expert to check the damp proof course.

To lower the moisture content, put the drawer in a warm, dry place for at least 24 hours.

3. A nail or screw, because of wear, may be protruding into the slide area. Pull the drawer out and inspect the slide assembly, using a torch if necessary. Remove the nail with pliers or pincers or take out the offending screw. If the drawers and runners have been glued, the removal of one fastener should cause no problem. If there is any doubt, put in another one where it will do no harm.

4. Too much friction between the drawer and runner (the member the drawer slides on) can make drawers difficult to operate. Rub on some dry lubricant (candle wax is good).

5. The drawer bottom, through overloading, may be sagging and rubbing on the drawer front beneath it. Depending on the drawer construction, you may be able to take out a few nails, slide the bottom out, and reverse it.

If the bottom is fully enclosed, simply place a piece of 50 x 18 mm dressed batten across the *inside* of the drawer and nail or screw the drawer bottom to it.

6. A worn drawer bottom or runner (or both) can cause jamming. If the runner is worn too severely, replace it with a new hardwood runner screwed to the side of the drawer (see Diagram 2). For a badly worn drawer bottom, plane it straight, then stick a thin strip of hardwood (or several strips of plastic laminate) to the bottom edges to build the drawer side up.

Repairing Coming-apart Drawers

The construction of most modern drawers is flimsy to say the least. Gone are the days when they were made with solid timber and the intricate, intriguing, interlocking dovetail joint. If your drawers are falling apart, nowadays the only solution is to reglue them.

PROCEDURE

1 Knock them apart using a hammer and a scrap block of wood. Or you can use a nail punch to remove the nails.

2 Clean off all the old glue and then, using some old newspaper to protect your working surface, liberally coat all joint surfaces with PVA glue (or use epoxy glue if you want super strength).

3 Reassemble the drawer and cramp it. Check the corners are at right angles by using a large set square (or simply make the diagonals equal). This is essential otherwise the drawer won't fit.

If you don't have a cramp, either nail the glued joints together with some 38 mm nails or stand the drawer on its end and lay some heavy books on the front. Wipe off the excess glue, allow to dry and then put the drawer back, sanding or planing it to fit as necessary.

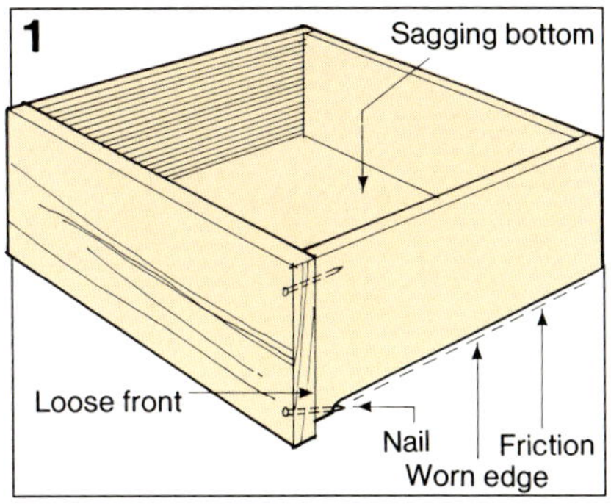

Diagram 1: a faulty drawer.

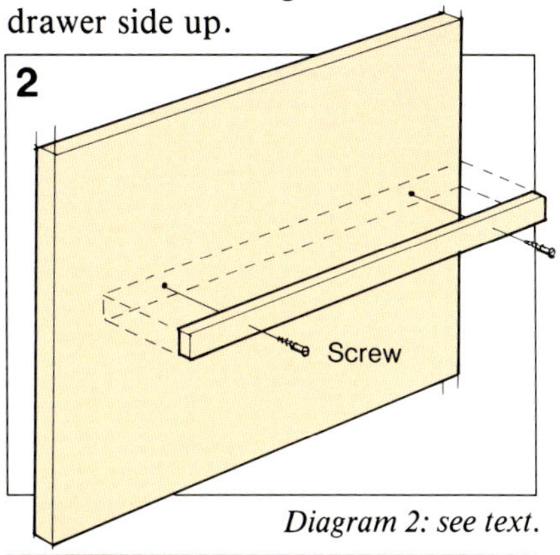

Diagram 2: see text.

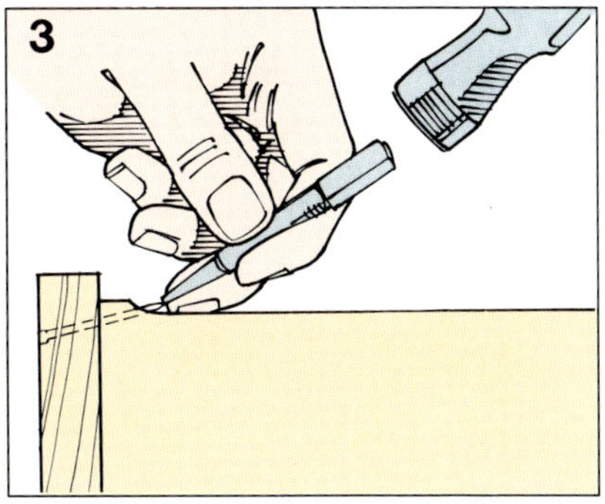

Diagram 3: removing a nail using a nail punch.

Diagram 4: if you don't have a cramp, lay some heavy books on the front.

Repairing Rotting Handrails or Door Frames

One of the enemies of timber is rot (see Repairing a Rotting Gate). In windows, door frames, handrails and posts, rotting is principally caused because the end grain of the timber has not been glued with a waterproof glue or properly primed with an oil-soluble primer. This oversight allows moisture to soak up the end grain of the timber and before you know it, the rotten little fungi begin their destructive cycle.

The sight of peeling or cracking paint around joint lines or near the bottoms of stiles or the tops of posts should alert you. Maple or oregon are susceptible but western red cedar is not. Push a penknife or skewer into the timber around the joint or end. If it's still solid, heave a sigh of relief, strip the paint off, then reprime, undercoat, and apply several finishing coats as quickly as possible so that further moisture can't get in.

If the knife blade sinks into the timber as it would a sponge cake, you've got real problems!

Depending on the extent of the rotting and the member it is affecting, you may be able to cut away the rotting section and glue a new piece in. Of course, if it's in more than one place, it would be better to replace the whole member.

Note that the joints used in window and door frames are usually housed, whereas handrail joints are either butted or mitred. The procedure for fixing them all is basically the same.

Door Stiles (or Handrail Posts)

The procedure for mending vertical members like door stiles or handrail posts is similar to Handrails. Pay special attention to the priming of the bottom of a jamb. Give it three coats of primer to make sure the problem doesn't recur. Then prime the rest of the new timber (plus any bare patches), undercoat, and apply two coats of water-soluble exterior grade paint.

If the jamb is loose, renail it into the timber framing.

Repairing Handrails

The rotting here is most likely to be found in the top of the posts or where the rails are joined.

PROCEDURE

1 Using a penknife or steel skewer, probe along the handrail until you locate solid timber. Then go another 300 mm and, using a square and sharp pencil, mark across the section.

2 To make a scarf joint, measure back 150 mm and mark again as in step 1. Then set up your gauge or combination square to half the thickness and mark both edges.

3 Make a series of saw cuts down to the gauge line. Ensure the two at either end are square both ways. Carefully following your lines will ensure this. Next chisel out the waste coming in from both sides. Don't take too much off at one go. When the waste is removed, check that the surface is level, using a square or the edge of your chisel.

4 Then cut the piece through and remove the rotten segment. Then simply repeat the scarfing process on the replacement piece leaving the other end long. When the scarf fits, cut the other end and fit it with your plane.

5 Glue or double prime the joint and fix together with galvanised nails or screws. A cramp will help to make it tight.

Push a steel skewer into the wood to test for rot.

Ants and fungi which have made a meal of this handrail are exposed.

Probe along the handrail until you locate solid timber.

Using a square and a sharp pencil, mark across the section.

Then go another 300 mm and mark again.

Set up your combination square to half the thickness and mark both edges.

Make a series of saw cuts down to the gauge line.

Chisel out the waste, coming in from both sides.

Check that the surface is level, using a square or the edge of your chisel.

Cut the piece through and remove the rotten segment.

Repeat the measuring and cutting on the replacement piece.

Try the new piece for size before gluing and nailing.

Spread glue on the joint.

Fix the joint with galvanised nails. A cramp will make it tight.

After the glue has dried, plane the edges of the rail smooth.

Finish by painting thoroughly to exclude damp.

Repairing Gypsum and Fibrous Plaster

Over-exuberance by children, or even over-indulgence by adults, could result in a gaping hole suddenly appearing in your gypsum plaster wall or ceiling (assuming, that is, there isn't the odd one already). Instead of hiding it with a pot plant, why don't you fix it? It's very simple to do — here's how.

Note: if your linings are fibrous plaster, the procedure for fixing a hole is somewhat similar — merely adjust the materials and jointing cements.

TOOLS AND MATERIALS

Some 120 grit sandpaper, saw, trimming knife, pencil and straight edge, a cork block, brushes or rollers and enough paint to do the patch or, better still, the wall, are needed.

Next obtain a straight-sided rectangular piece of gypsum plaster that is slightly larger than the hole. However, don't buy a full sheet! You may be able to get a small piece off a building site or an offcut from a firm that installs gypsum plaster. Make sure the piece is the same thickness as the existing wall lining.

You will also need some cornice cement, plus jointing cement, self-sticking jointing tape, broadknives (some suppliers sell a cheap package which includes one plastic 100 mm, one 150 mm and one 200 mm).

PROCEDURE

You will see that the piece of gypsum plaster has a white core (of calcined gypsum) with a paper linerboard on both sides. It is important you don't damage or scuff this paper lining by oversanding it otherwise your paint finish will be second-rate. Cutting the gypsum plaster can be done either by deeply scoring it with a trimming knife and then snapping the piece away from the cut, or by using a fine handsaw.

1 Lay the piece over the hole (making sure it's reasonably level) and mark around the perimeter. Using a straight edge, draw lines to represent the diagonals, as shown in the picture.

2 With a fine handsaw, cut from the hole along the diagonals into each corner.

3 Then, using your trimming knife and a small straight edge (steel is best), cut deeply around the edges of the rectangle. Keep outside the lines by about 2 mm to make sure that the patch will fit. Snap the pieces out by bending them *away* from the cut face.

4 From the offcuts, make four small blocks (two for smaller holes) approximately 100 × 100 mm. Stick them in position with the cornice cement and allow an hour or so for them to dry completely.

5 Next, push the replacement piece, face out, into place, making sure you put a liberal amount of cornice cement on the blocks. Allow to dry.

6 Sand the painted wall around the patch for a distance equal to at least 300 mm. This will allow the jointing cement to key.

7 Next, stick on the tape and cover with a thin layer of jointing cement 100 mm wide (the tape works in the joint like reinforcing steel in concrete). Allow to dry for 24 hours. Sand off any irregularities, then follow up with a thin layer of cement about 300 mm wide, then, after another 24 hours, one 600 mm wide. Feather the edges off to nothing on the painted section each time. If possible, cover the whole area of the patch with jointing cement.

8 When dry, sand thoroughly, brush all the dust off the surface (otherwise the paint might lift), paint the area with an approved sealer, and finish the wall with a matching paint.

If you've followed the steps carefully and neatly, no one, including you, will ever believe there was a hole there.

The problem: a gaping hole in a gypsum plaster wall.

Lay a piece of plaster over the hole and mark round it.

Cut from the hole along the diagonals you have drawn.

Cut round the edges of the rectangle with a trimming knife.

Make two small blocks from the offcuts and stick them in place.

Push the replacement piece, face out, into position.

Sand the painted wall around the patch for at least 300 mm.

Stick on the jointing tape and cover with a layer of cement.

Allow to dry for 24 hours and sand off any irregularities.

Apply a thin layer of cement about 300 mm wide.

Sand the area again and feather the edges off to nothing.

Paint the area with an approved sealer before painting the wall.

Regrouting a Leaking Shower Recess

A leak in a shower recess may be caused by nothing more than the grout having deteriorated. Grout (the material which fills the joints between the tiles) can dry out and crack. Continual exposure to water may also leach out the grout's waterproofing qualities. The result, especially where the walls are brick, can be dampness leading to a breakdown in the paint on the other side of the wall, which often shows up as a peeling or powdering patch in an adjoining room.

The best solution to the problem is to regrout the tile joints to stop the seepage, assuming the problem is not caused by a leak in the plumbing or a breakdown in the flashing between the shower recess floor and walls. Both of these problems require professional attention.

A shower recess showing grouting which has deteriorated.

A close-up of the faulty grouting.

Rake out the joints with a tungsten-tipped grout raker.

Force the new grout into the joints with a broad knife.

Wipe off the excess grout with a dampened sponge.

TOOLS AND MATERIALS

You'll require sufficient grout to cover the area of tiles (choose a colour to blend or contrast with the tiles and remember white is the most difficult to keep clean). Make sure you tell your supplier what size the tiles are — smaller tiles have more joints.

While you're at the hardware store, buy a tungsten-tipped grout raker. It makes short work of raking out the joints (it's claimed to take around three hours to do a twelve square metre area) and is far safer to use than a screwdriver which will damage or chip the edges of the tiles.

Besides the raker, you'll need some old sheets or blankets to cover the bath and basin, a putty or broad knife, a sponge, an old ceramic dish to mix the grout in, a rainy day and a good sporting event or orchestral concert to listen to.

PROCEDURE

1 Lay the padding over the important items. Either have bare feet or wear soft-soled shoes. Angle the rake into a joint, and, making sure you follow the line of the joint, begin to remove the old grout. Ideally, you must create a cavity at least 1.5 mm in depth by the full width of the joint. Work from the top down and towards the light so that no joints are missed. Be especially careful to create a joint where the tiles join the bath or vanity top and at the bottom of the shower recess. These are two notorious spots for leakages.

2 Clean up the old grout that you've raked out. Then simply mix up the new grout and force it into the joints with the putty or broad knife. Use the slightly dampened sponge to smooth it off and remove the excess. When it's dry, polish the tiles. The bad patch of paint in the next room should be rectified when the wall is thoroughly dry.

Replacing a Flush Cone

Does a mysterious pool of water appear behind the toilet every time you flush the cistern? Don't blame your kids! It could be that the flush cone, the rubber seal that fits over the back of most pans, has perished and is leaking.

One thing is certain — the problem will get worse and worse. Why not replace the seal? It's not a difficult or dirty job (the water is clean) and you'll save money and a lot of inconvenience.

Turn off the stop tap to prevent the cistern filling.

TOOLS AND MATERIALS

Before you begin, check the diameter of the flush pipe, the L-shaped pipe that fits between the cistern and the pan. Then toddle off to your friendly hardware store and get a new flush cone.

You may only need a wrench to loosen the nut that secures the flush pipe to the cistern. If the flush pipe is metal you should also get some thread tape to reseal the joint.

PROCEDURE

1 Turn off the stop tap (the tap that regulates the water supply to the cistern), then flush the toilet. This is in case the flush button is accidentally pushed during the operation and your bathroom floor suffers a flood.

2 Unscrew the nut at the top of the flush pipe.

3 Locate where the rubber seal fits over the horn at the back of the pan then, using your fingers, roll the edge of the rubber back (it's like rolling down a pair of socks or stockings) until the flush pipe comes free.

4 Remove the old flush cone and clean the pipe.

5 Slip the new flush cone over the end of the pipe (wetting the pipe with detergent will help), and then roll the rubber back over itself, inverting it.

6 Push the end of the flush pipe firmly into the opening in the pan, then loosely tighten the top nut.

7 Roll the seal over the outside of the pan horn, then tighten the nut, resealing it if it's metal.

8 Turn on the stop tap, let the cistern fill up with water and then push the button.

If things pan out for you, you will be flushed with success. If the water persists, call a plumber!

Unscrew the nut at the top of the flush pipe.

Roll back the rubber seal until the flush pipe comes free.

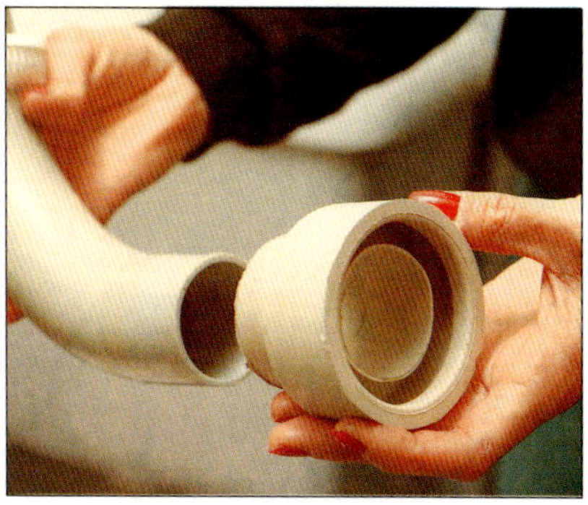

After cleaning the pipe, slip the new flush cone over the end.

Roll the rubber back over itself, inverting it.

Roll the seal over the outside of the horn at the back of the pan.

The new flush cone in place — no more leaks!

Repairing a Leaking Roof

A leaking roof, which is evidenced by damp ceilings or water runs down a wall, may be caused by cracked tiles, leaking flashings, rusted valley gutters, or capillary action between the overlapping joints in corrugated iron.

Repairing Flashing

Where various projections such as chimneys or vents poke through your roof, a flashing is used. This is often lead because lead is heavy and its softness enables it to be worked so it fits the shape of the tiles, corrugated iron or the roundness of the vent. However, because of electrolysis, sometimes other materials are used.

Over time and with continual thermal contraction and expansion, the joint between the flashing and the roof surface or vent sometimes leaks. You notice it when drops of water run down the pipe inside your house or when the paint peels off near a chimney.

Get up on the roof and check the flashings are still fitting tightly against both the roof surface and the projection. If the flashing has lifted in a wind or there is evidence of water getting in underneath it, buy some roof caulking compound from your hardware store and, with a putty knife, spread some over the joint. Then press the flashing back down, tapping it lightly into shape with a wooden block. If the flashing has cracked with age it's best to get in a tradesperson to replace it.

If the flashing collar around a vent is leaking, apply a liberal amount of caulking around the top joint. If that doesn't work, call in a plumber.

Making Corrugated Iron Waterproof

Water can get up between tightly fitting sheets of corrugated iron by either capillary action or through the driving force of the wind. If there is evidence of water leaking from around the over-lapping joints in the sheets you may have to undo the screws and, using a suitable caulking compound or silicone sealer, fill the joint, then screw the sheets back down. While you're at it, check that the water isn't coming in through the screw holes. If it is, replace the washers.

When walking on corrugated iron, make sure you put your feet on the area adjacent to the screw holes. This is where the supporting battens are. If you walk in between the battens, you run the risk that you'll permanently distort the sheeting. Should the iron be a bit rusty, you could also go through it.

Evidence of a leaking roof: a damp patch on a ceiling.

Flashing round a projection in a roof may lift in the wind.

Spread some roof caulking compound over the joint.

Press the flashing back down, tapping it with a wooden block.

If the flashing collar round a vent is leaking, apply caulking.

The cracked tile which is causing the leak will be fairly obvious.

Lift the front of the row above it and hold in place with blocks.

Slip in the replacement tile, using a twisting motion.

Make sure the new tile fits neatly and lower the higher row.

Replacing a Cracked Tile

You'll often discover the existence of a cracked roof tile when you see a damp spot on your ceiling or the paint starts peeling off in just one place. Hopefully the builders have left some spare tiles under your house for this emergency. If they haven't, and the house is fairly new, you should be able to get some the same from the manufacturer. If it's a discontinued style or the house is old you may have to search secondhand building supply yards.

PROCEDURE

With a replacement tile and a couple of offcuts of 50 x 25 mm batten, carefully proceed to the approximate position of the leak, making sure you walk on the noses of the tiles (their front edge). The cracked tile should be fairly obvious unless it's a hairline crack.

Lift the front of the row above it and hold in place with the blocks. Remove the pieces of tile. If the tile is nailed to the fixing batten, simply lever the piece upwards. The top piece has a lip which must be lifted over the batten to allow removal. If it is wired or the nail won't budge, smash the tile and remove the fastening with a pair of pliers.

Proceed to slip in the replacement using a twisting motion. Make sure it fits neatly, then lower the higher row. This will lock it in place and if all goes well end the problem forever.

LADDER SAFETY

Getting up on the roof to fix the problem involves using a ladder. They are potentially dangerous if not used correctly. When using a step ladder, make sure you stand it on a surface that is level and firm and spread the legs widely.

With an extension ladder, the correct slope should be one in four. This means that the feet of the ladder should be placed outside the gutter line a distance equal to one quarter of the height between the ground and the gutter (see Diagram). Also the top of the ladder should extend at least one metre above the roof line and the top half of the ladder should not be extended more than three-quarters of its length.

Again make sure the extension ladder stands on a firm surface. With both ladders, get someone to hold them while you ascend and descend. Wear shoes with soles that grip (like sandshoes), and wait until the roof is dry before you get up on it.

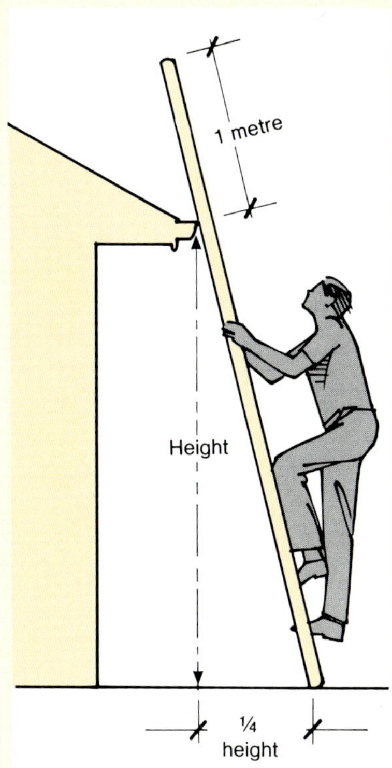

The correct slope for an extension ladder is one in four.

Fixing Wooden Furniture

Over time, excessive wear or poor construction can result in loose-jointed furniture. Other problems that can occur are splits, wobbly legs, rocking tables or chairs, and a breakdown of the finish.

Wobbly Legs

Sometimes legs are affixed to a table or chair simply by brackets or screwed blocks. Look under your table or chair to see if the screws have come loose. First try tightening them up. If they keep turning, then remove them and, buying a slightly larger diameter screw, rescrew them. If the timber is split or the hole too large, then fill the hole with glue and wooden matches. Allow to dry; then rescrew.

Other common joints used in furniture construction are dowelled or mortice and tenon. The best way to fix a loose joint is to knock it apart, clean off the old glue with a file, rasp or sandpaper, then glue (epoxy for clear finishes or PVA for painted) and cramp the article back together again. Make sure it is square and in wind. In wind means the leg or arm, when sighted, lines up with the other ones.

However, before resorting to this drastic step, if the article is painted, first try pouring and rubbing a liquid glue (PVA) into all sides of the offending joint. If all goes well, capillary action will pull enough glue in to hold it. You may also be able to screw a 75 mm metal bracket to the inside of the joint to increase the strength.

If, when you pull the joint apart, you find the dowel or tenon broken, replace it. With dowels simply cut them off flush and then, using a 2 mm drill bit, bore a pilot hole through their centre. Then, using a bit the same size as the dowel, drill out the old dowels, and replace them with new ones.

If the tenon has broken, cut it off flush, rip 50 mm into the member in the same line as the old tenon and chisel out the piece. Then fit and glue a false tenon in position (see diagram). When the glue has dried, fit and reglue the joint.

Rocking Tables or Chairs

Assuming the joints are firm, rocking is caused by legs that have worn unevenly or bowed and are therefore different lengths.

To fix this, select a dead flat surface such as a table (cover it first with newspaper to lessen damage) or a well-laid floor. Pack the two short legs with equal amounts of coins until the table is absolutely steady. Then take a sharp pencil and, laying it hard against the surface, run a line around each leg. With a tenon saw, cut each leg neatly to this line. If there is only a tiny bit to cut off, use coarse sandpaper and a block, or a flat file.

Split Members

A properly glued split should result in the timber being at least as strong as it was before the split, if not stronger. Use epoxy glue for maximum strength. Simply open the split up (or separate the two pieces completely), coat both surfaces with glue, bring them together, and then secure with a cramp until the glue has set. Wipe off the excess glue — otherwise you'll have a long job sanding it back. Be careful not to get the glue on your skin — it's dangerous.

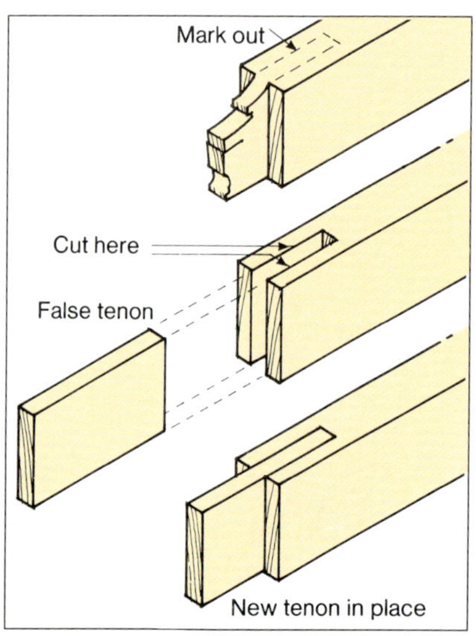

If a tenon has broken you can replace it with a false tenon.

A rickety old table sadly in need of repair.

Open up splits and then coat both surfaces with glue.

Secure joints with a clamp until the glue has dried.

To fix a rocking table pack the two short legs with coins.

Use an old toothbrush to apply stripper on moulded legs.

Fill any gaps with wood putty of an appropriate colour.

Lay a pencil against the floor and run a line round each leg.

Cut each leg neatly to this line with a tenon saw.

Renewing Poor Finishes

To achieve a good result, the old finish must be removed. This involves stripping. Proper stripping requires infinite patience, especially on turned or moulded members. If the item is a valuable antique, it could pay you to get an expert to do it for you.

To select the right stripper you first have to identify the old finish. Paint and varnish are easy. They can be removed with liquid, paste or water-rinse strippers. Shellac will dissolve if you apply some methylated spirits. Lacquer requires lacquer thinners. A half-shellac, half-lacquer finish requires fifty per cent of each of their solvents.

TOOLS AND MATERIALS

The appropriate stripper plus plenty of newspaper, an old brush, a paint scraper such as a Skarsten, a stainless steel pot scourer, some steel wool, an old toothbrush, gloves and long protective clothing, sandpaper and cork block.

PROCEDURE

1 Select a day when your biorhythm is in an up cycle. If using stripper, take the item out on a verandah or to an open garage. Good ventilation is essential.

2 Read the stripper directions carefully. With all your skin covered, liberally brush on the stripper in 300 mm squares (or 300 mm lengths on legs and rails, etc.), and leave for the required time. On flat surfaces, begin to scrape (or hose) off the wrinkled paint, keeping the tool at a low angle so it doesn't dig in.

3 If using methylated spirits or thinners, keep re-applying it. This gradually melts the old finish. Remove each sticky layer using a plentiful supply of clean rags. On curved or moulded legs, use a scourer, rasp or the toothbrush. (Watch the bristles don't flick the stripper in your eyes.) Finish off with steel wool. A small screwdriver is handy for getting into tight corners. A piece of coarse string or strip of old carpet looped around a curved leg and energetically pulled back and forth will entice the old finish off. When it's finished, it is important to neutralise the stripper otherwise the new finish could peel off. Be especially finicky at this stage and follow the directions carefully. If the old finish is not entirely removed, repeat the operation entirely or just redo the stubborn patches.

4 Then fill any holes and sand the job with coarse and then fine sandpaper (always working with the grain). Dust off, and then carefully apply the new finish in accordance with the manufacturer's directions.

Eliminating Draughts

Eliminating draughts will make your home or unit more comfortable during the cold months of winter. While there are other things you can do such as installing combustion stoves or gas heaters, putting down carpets, covering windows with heavy drapes, installing skylights, insulating your ceiling and trimming trees that block the northerly sun, lessening chilling winter draughts will help. Keep in mind, however, that some fresh air is essential for good health.

Sealing Strips

For starters, you can put stick-on sealing strips around all ill-fitting doors and casement window rebates. These easily installed heat savers are sold by the metre or in rolls, so simply measure the length around each rebate and total them up. You'll need some methylated spirits and a rag to clean the rebates thoroughly, plus a sharp knife.

Open the ill-fitting window or door as wide as possible and clean the rebate thoroughly. Measure and cut each piece to length and *then* pull off the backing and stick it on. There is no need to do the area on the side of the casement stays as, if they have been fitted properly, there is hardly any gap there to allow a draught in.

Caulking Gaps

Finish off your draught proofing by caulking all draught-creating external openings such as those that occur under window sills, around plumbing pipes, etc. For most applications, silicone is ideal although, as with draught excluders, there are other products on the market. Select a caulking compound that is weather-resistant, non-drying, non-shrinking, and adheres to most materials. If you want the caulking to be inconspicuous then choose one in a matching or neutral colour or one that can be painted over. If you have a lot of sealing to do, a caulking gun makes the job much easier.

Stick on sealing strips round ill-fitting doors and windows.

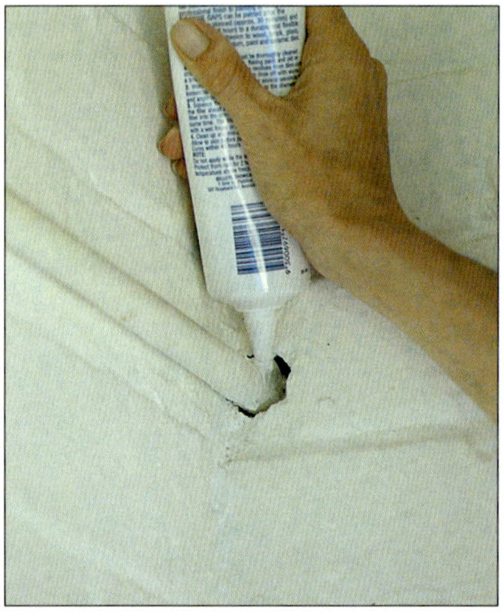

Fill in gaps round pipes with caulking compound.

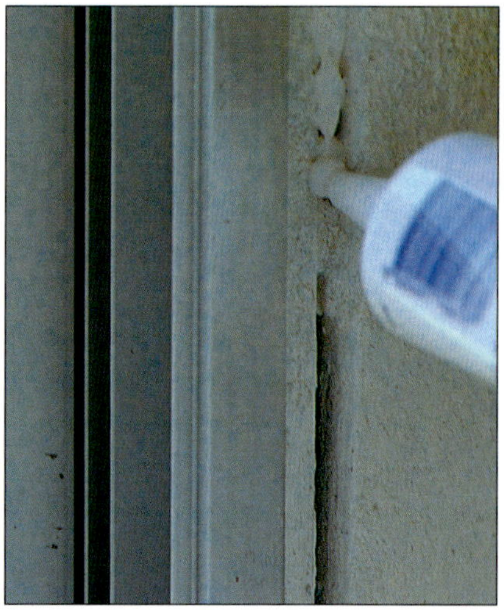

Caulking compound can also be used for gaps beside windows or doors.

To fit a draught deflector, measure the door width.

Cut the draught deflector to length with a hacksaw.

Use a nail punch to mark the screw holes in the door.

First check the outside walls and note all positions where gaps occur (around windows, door frames, water pipes, etc.). Then cut the top off the conical cap and squeeze the compound into position. Smooth off the joint with your thumb. Remove any surplus with a rag dipped in the recommended cleaner. If you are worried about getting a smear of caulking on bricks, etc. put some masking tape around the area, apply the sealer, then simply peel the tape off. If you're painting the caulking, allow the surface to cure a little.

Fitting Draught Deflectors

An effective step in eliminating draughts is to fit draught (which may also be water) deflectors to the bottom of external doors, especially those facing south or west. These come in many types. Discuss your particular location with your hardware storeperson but remember to take along details such as which side the door is hinged (looking from the outside), what type of tread under the door you have, and the door width.

TOOLS

You'll need a hacksaw (to cut the deflector to length), hand drill and drill bits to suit the screws, screwdriver, and a tape and pencil. If you have a terrazzo tread and you purchase a deflector that has a sill, you may need a masonry bit and some plugs to fix the sill in position.

PROCEDURE

1 Measure the door width and cut the strip to length.

2 With the door closed, position the deflector above the tread and mark the screw holes.

3 Drill a hole of a diameter equal to the solid part of the thread or use a nail punch.

4 Screw the fitting on the door with two screws, check for fit, and then complete. The sill, if any, is fitted similarly.

Insulating a Ceiling

Insulating ceilings is like putting a thick blanket over each room. It seals the warmth in and keeps the cold out. It cuts heat loss by 50% while the cost is small. For an average home, $500–$700 should cover it. This is not expensive if you keep in mind that you could well achieve a thirty per cent saving to your winter heating bills. The house will be cooler in summer, too.

If you're handy, agile, sure that the wiring in the roof is safe, and the roof is of high enough pitch, you could insulate the ceilings yourself (and save around $125.00).

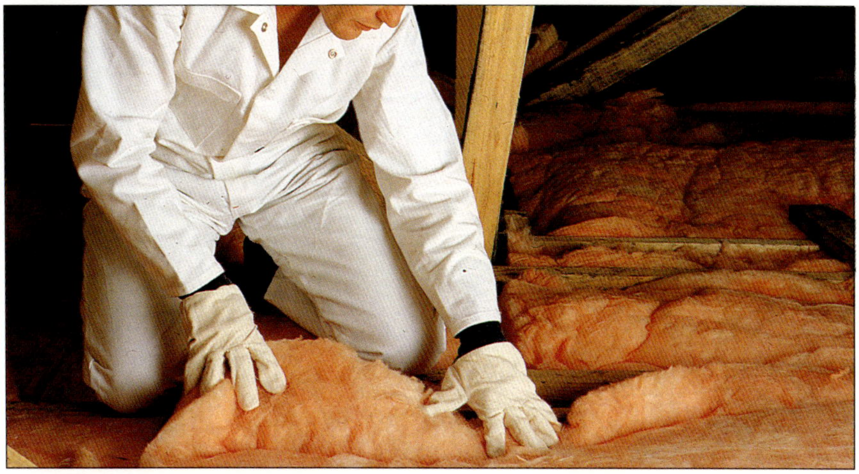

Wearing protective clothing, pack the batts lightly between the joists.

TOOLS AND MATERIALS

Simply calculate the floor area and, getting in through the access hole, measure the average distance between the ceiling joists. Your insulation supplier will calculate the quantity of batts required and the size.

With the batts, a ladder, lead light, a trimming knife (for cutting the batts to size), gloves, a paper particle mask, long-sleeved shirt and long trousers (the insulation can irritate your skin and nasal passages), and two pieces of metre square 18 mm ply or particle board for cutting and kneeling on, you're ready to go. If the roof is a trussed one, use a plank that spans at least four of the chords to spread your weight.

PROCEDURE

1 Choose a cool day (otherwise you'll dehydrate) and begin packing the batts tightly between the joists, making sure you reach right to the external wall plate. Work back toward the access hole. Leave no spaces for maximum effect. Always keep your weight on the joists and not on the ceiling! The short plank or ply square will made the procedure more comfortable.

2 If the pitch is low, a 75 mm slat of wood that just fits between the joists should be fixed to the end of a broom handle. That will provide a useful pushing tool for moving the batts into awkward places.

Be especially careful around any wiring. A stiff cardboard separator should be used to isolate the wire from the insulation material.

Keep the material 100 mm clear of chimneys and flues. Don't forget to cover the access hole but don't block off any ceiling fans, etc.

3 You could, if you have uncarpeted floors, put batts between the floor joists to effect another 10% heating saving.

Let winter come now. Your home is snug! In summer it will be much cooler, too.

Replacing Plastic Laminate

Plastic laminate provides a serviceable and attractive finish for kitchen and vanity bench tops. It excels where moisture is present.

However, over time, the surface may become damaged by normal wear and tear or scratched by the use of over-harsh powder cleaners. Also the pattern and colour may become dated. Why not replace the tops and edging? You can do this by simply gluing new laminate on top of the old.

The first step is to sand all surfaces thoroughly.

To cut the edge strips, score heavily with a laminate cutter.

TOOLS AND MATERIALS

You'll need a laminate cutter, a sharp plane, a straight edge, a large flat file (unless you can hire a laminate trimmer), some wooden dowels or slats for separators, tape and pencil, and a square.

Make an accurate plan of the tops and edges so your supplier can help you work out how much laminate and glue you need (keep the figuring so you can cut the sheets correctly). When you make your selection, remember that what looks good in a small sample often looks terrible en masse. Be smart and try to see your choice in someone else's house first.

The adhesive normally used is a rubber-based contact glue (see Glues). For a good job, the existing tops must be solidly bonded and all lifting edges must be reglued (see Lifting and Bubbling Laminate).

Heavily sand all surfaces.

PROCEDURE FOR EDGE STRIPPING

1 Carefully (it is easily cracked) lay the sheet, pattern up, on a table and, using a soft pencil, mark out the required width (make it 1.5 mm wider). Make sure you cut the edge strips from the area designated for them.

2 Lay the straight edge along the line and score heavily with the laminate cutter until much of the brown undersurface shows through.

3 Hold the straight edge hard down on top of the laminate directly alongside the cut and, working from one end, carefully lift the edge until the strip cracks off. Repeat until you have all the edge strips.

4 Now cut the strips to length making them 1.5 mm longer than the finished length. Apply contact glue to both surfaces and wait until it's touch dry. Now to the tricky part. It's essential to line them up correctly first time (for long pieces, get a friend to help you). Making it flush with the bottom, push one end into place, then work along to the other end pressing it on as you go. Then go back and tap the strip firmly with a hammer and block. Continue with the other strips and, when finished, leave to dry for an hour or so.

5 Trim the strips flush with the top and on the ends using the flat file, plane, or the electric laminate trimmer (which you should set up and try out on a scrap piece first). When filing, hold the file flat and make sure you file away from the finished surface or you might chip it. The plane is much faster than the file but the laminate eventually takes the edge off it, necessitating more frequent sharpening.

PROCEDURE FOR BENCH TOPS

1 Check whether the benches are square, parallel and at right angles to each other and then mark out and cut the tops, allowing at least 2 mm extra all around. If the bench has a flush or circular sink in it, unscrew the plumbing and the sink clips and lift the sink out rather than try to fit the laminate to it.

Using your plane, fit the top to the bench. Laying the sheet on a table so it projects slightly past it is the best way to plane it.

2 When it fits, apply the glue as before. Then, after it's touch dry, lay the separators on the surface and position the top accurately (see illustration). Slide each separator out (beginning from one end to avoid trapping any air) and when stuck down, tap all over with the block and hammer as before.

3 Trim the excess off with your file or plane (or use a laminate trimmer with a bevelled cutter), making sure you don't damage the edge strips. Incline either tool at 45° to get rid of the sharp edges. Clean off the glue with the correct solvent and give the surface a wipe over.

Looks terrific, doesn't it? If you're feeling especially confident and you want to complete the kitchen transformation, why not do the doors as well?

Hold the straight edge down and carefully lift the edge strip.

Apply contact glue to both the bench edge and the new strip.

Apply the edge strip making it flush with the bottom.

Tap the strip firmly with a hammer and block.

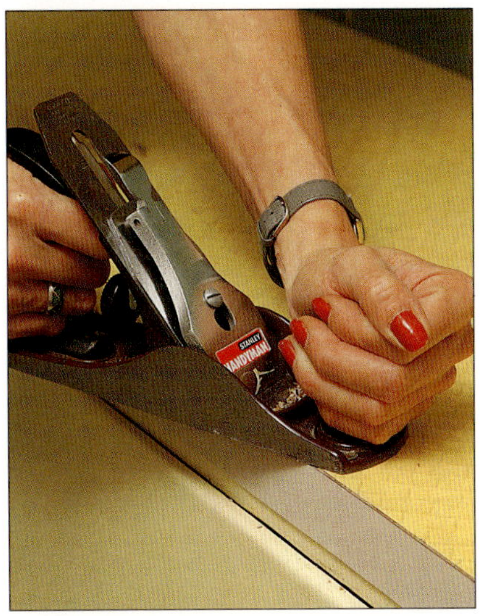

Trim the strip flush with the top using a plane.

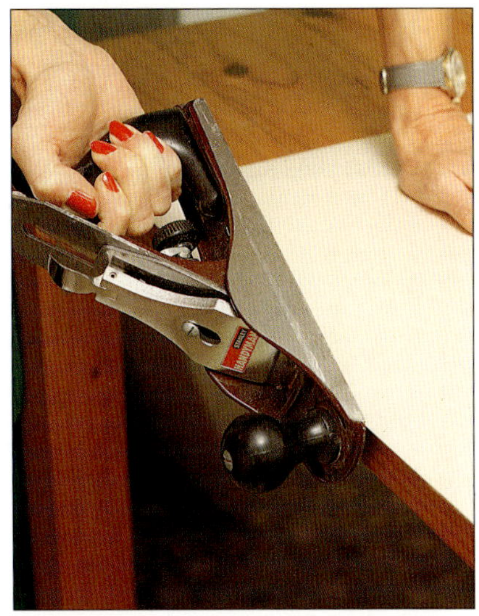

Using a plane, fit the top to the bench.

Apply the contact glue to both surfaces.

Lay the separators on the surface and position the top.

Plane off the excess and finish off with a file. Don't damage the edge strips.

Removing a Cracked Tile

There's nothing more unsightly than a cracked tile in a bathroom floor or on the kitchen wall. It gathers dirt in the crevice, boldly outlining its presence for all your fastidious friends to see. It is also a repository for germs.

Removing it (or a tile that has previously had a fitting screwed to it) is not the impossible task it appears. But whatever you do, *don't* try to lever the offending tile out with a screwdriver or knife. Instead of having to replace one tile you'll end up having to replace a few hundred!

Getting the tile out is easy enough if you follow the steps below. Finding an exact replacement may prove to be more difficult. If the tile you need is out of production and possible replacements are of a slightly different colour, perhaps you could put in a fancy feature tile that has harmonious or contrasting tones. A scout around the tile shops will, I'm sure, result in the discovery of a satisfactory replacement.

There are samples of some of the many tiles available on page 76.

Rake out the grout so that the cracked tile is separated completely from the surrounding tiles.

TOOLS AND MATERIALS

You need a grout rake (which costs only a few dollars), a hammer, fine cold chisel, large screwdriver, putty knife, sponge and polishing rag. If the tile is undamaged except for a hairline crack you'll also need a hand or electric drill (an electric drill is easier) and a small masonry bit.

As for materials, a small amount of tile adhesive (or sand and cement if you're going to lay the tile with mortar), some flexible grout of a matching colour plus a couple of tile spacers should suffice. If the rest of the grouting is hard and cracked, perhaps you should consider raking out all the joints and regrouting the whole area before too much moisture gets behind the tiles and threatens to loosen them. (See Regrouting a Leaking Shower Recess.)

PROCEDURE

1 Cover any bath, basin or vanity top with an old blanket in case you accidentally damage them by dropping one of the tools. Then carefully rake out the grout so that the tile is completely isolated from its companions.

2 Unless the tile already has a hole in it, insert the masonry bit tightly in the drill chuck and drill a hole in the centre of the tile.

3 Working outwards from the centre and taking small bites each time, carefully chip out the tile using the hammer and cold chisel. Make sure you wear safety glasses of some sort to avoid getting razor sharp tile chips in your eyes! Also, when sweeping up the debris, watch that you don't cut your fingers.

4 When the tile is out, carefully clean around the edges and then prepare the undersurface for the new tile. This may involve levelling the surface, sealing porous materials such as gypsum plaster, and making sure that the area is clean, dry and solid (see Replacing a Few Ceramic Tiles).

5 Using a generous amount of tile adhesive, glue the replacement tile back in position. For rendered walls, a 4:1 cement and sand mortar is adequate. Check that the tile is exactly in line with the existing ones and that the joint around it is even. If it goes in too far, pull it out and use more adhesive or mortar.

6 When dry, regrout the joint. Remember to wipe the grout off the tile face *before* it dries. A quick polish with a clean rag will blend the new tile in nicely.

Start from the centre. Bore a hole in the tile if necessary.

Carefully chip out the tile with hammer and cold chisel.

When the tile is out, carefully clean round the edges.

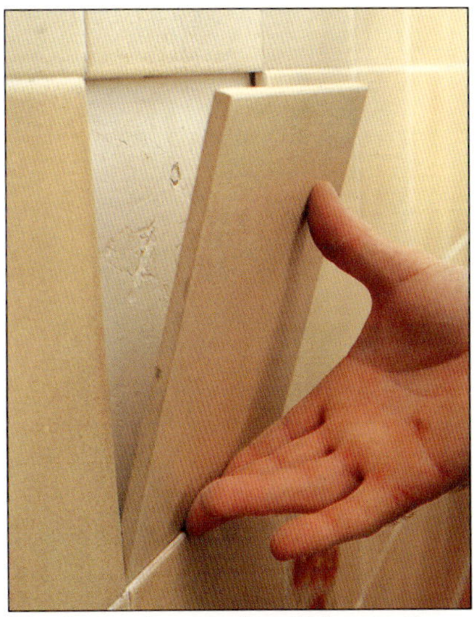
Check that the new tile will fit into the gap.

Spread adhesive on the back of the new tile.

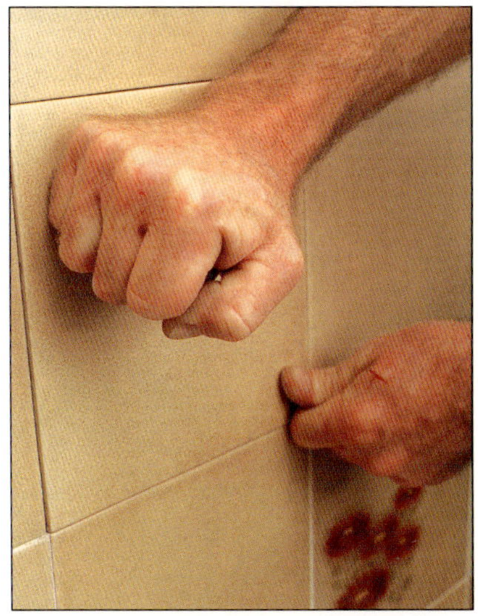
Press the new tile firmly into position.

When the adhesive is dry, regrout the joint.

Wipe off excess grout with a damp sponge.

Polish the tile with a clean cloth or rag.

Patching Rendering

Rendered walls or columns give a very serviceable surface. But occasionally, because of dirty or dusty surface, or because of a poorly mixed batch of mortar, or as a result of the wall getting heavily bumped, or the reinforcing steel rusting, the rendering comes off.

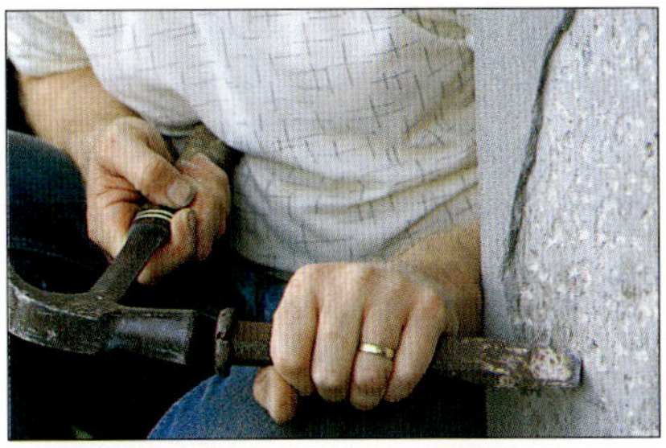

Sparrow pick the concrete where the render is missing.

Wet the patch thoroughly before applying the new render.

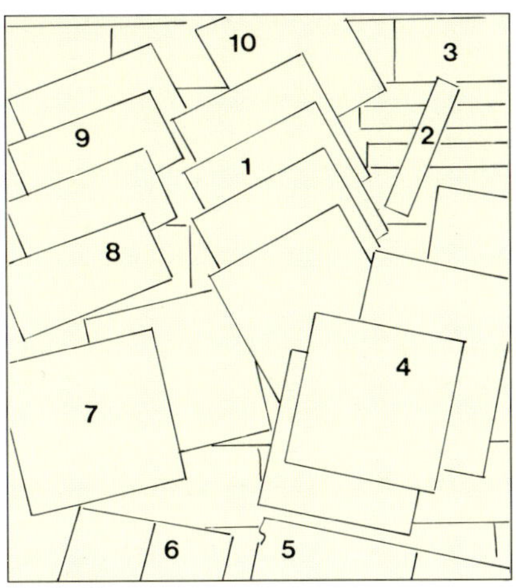

Wall tiles
1. *Plain square tiles*
2. *Narrow edge trims*
3. *Plain white oblong tiles*
4. *Square patterned tiles*
5. *Edge trim tiles*
6. *Plain coloured oblong tiles*
7. *Reproduction old-fashioned feature tiles*
8. *Printed tiles, Art Nouveau designs*
9. *Handpainted tiles* 10. *Feature tile*

Begin to fill the patch working from the bottom up.

Leave it to set a little and then finish off with a float.

TOOLS AND MATERIALS

You'll need sufficient sand and cement for the job using a 3:1 mix. (A mixture of one part of cement, one of lime and eight of sand is better for concrete block walls.) The sand should be suitable for rendering, with little loam in it. Your material supplier should know what is required. As a rough guide, 0.125 m^3 sand and 40 kg cement will make up 4 m^2 of mortar approximately 10 mm thick.

Most rendered walls or columns are finished with a wooden float. This gives a coarse, grainy finish. If they are very smooth, either they have been painted a number of times (possible in older houses) or a steel float has been used.

You'll also need a straight edge which is longer than the widest part of the patch, a hammer and cold chisel (or scutch), a shovel for mixing, a bucket and brush for wetting the wall, and a hawk. This is not a raptorial bird, but a 300 × 300 mm piece of 10 mm ply. In its centre is fixed a wooden handle. You use this hand-held platform for holding the mortar while you scoop some up and press it up the wall with the underside of the float.

PROCEDURE

1 Chop around the edge of the patch with a hammer and cold chisel to make sure there is no more drumminess (loose render) on the wall.

2 Use a scutch or the hammer and cold chisel to sparrow pick the brickwork or concrete where the rendering has come loose to increase adhesion on the subsurface. When you have finished, clean the surface of any oil and make sure it is dust free. If you still have doubts about the surface, use something like Bondcrete in the mix to increase adhesion.

3 Next, lay some old carpet or boards on the floor to catch the mortar droppings. Wet the patch thoroughly before you begin to mix up the ingredients. The mix should be pliable but not sloppy.

4 Transfer some mortar to the hawk with the float. Lay the hawk back towards you, cut away some render with the trowel, and begin to fill the patch working from the bottom up. When it's covered, if the area is large, use the straight edge in a back and forth motion to cut away the excess mortar.

5 Go back over the patch and fill any low spots, then again screed it with the straight edge or float.

6 Leave it to set a little, then go over it with the float (wood or steel) to finish it off.

Before you paint it, allow to dry for at least four weeks (a heater could accelerate the drying), then seal and paint. For best results, do the whole wall or the paint finish could be patchy.

Relaying Loose Bricks

Brickwork relies for its strength on having a good underlying foundation, a properly constructed footing, and a strong mortar bonding the bricks together. However, given that imperfect human beings are involved in all construction work, sometimes a few bricks can come loose. Why not relay them? A few hours' work could return the wall or fence to its original glory (assuming the problem is a minor one). Besides, once you have laid a few bricks and got the knack, you may end up building barbecues, retaining walls . . . who knows where it could end? Look at the Great Wall of China!

HANDY HINT

If you've been a little overzealous with the mortar and managed to spread it over much of the brickwork then it should be cleaned off immediately. Use a wet brush and scrub as much away as you can without wetting the joints (this will wash the cement out).

If when the mortar has dried the stains are still evident, wet the area thoroughly, then clean the bricks with a brush and diluted mixture of hydrochloric acid and water (1 acid : 15 of water is suitable or 1:10 at most). Leave the acid on the bricks for 5 minutes maximum to stop it soaking into the brick and then hose off, using plenty of water. Take care to cover your skin as the acid burns.

TOOLS AND MATERIALS

You'll need sufficient sand (of a type suitable for making mortar), cement, lime (this makes the mortar easier to use) plus perhaps a suitable oxide to colour the mortar to match the existing joints. A good, general purpose mortar mix is 1 part cement: 1 part lime: 6 parts sand measured by volume. For areas below the damp proof course where strength and waterproofness is important, a 1 part cement to 3 parts of sand mix with just a smidgen of lime is ideal. The mortar, when mixed, should have a thick, paste-like consistency.

You'll need a lump hammer (although an ordinary hammer will do), a bolster or comb chisel for cleaning off the old mortar (a cold chisel or old wood chisel might just suffice), a shovel, trowel, level, and perhaps a tool for ironing (making a rounded joint) or raking (making a square joint) to match the shape of the existing brick joints.

PROCEDURE

1 Clean the old mortar off the bricks (both the loose ones and their solidly bonded neighbours) with the hammer and comb chisel. Put the loose bricks on a layer of sand while you're chopping away to lessen the chance of cracking them. Don't damage the DPC (damp proof course, the impervious, continuous layer built into a brick joint to stop moisture from the ground travelling up the wall) should you meet it.

2 When the bricks are clean, wet them either in a bucket of water or by hosing (but don't saturate them). Hose the place where they will be laid as well. This will stop the bricks sucking the moisture out of the mortar too quickly and make it adhere to the bricks better.

3 Measure out the different parts of the ingredients (an ice-cream container will make sure you get the correct volumes of each) and thoroughly mix them with the shovel. Select a waterproof surface to mix on otherwise your cement will soak away.

4 Make a hole in the centre of the mortar (rather like a volcano crater) and begin to add the water. Don't allow it to flood or you'll lose some of the cement and affect the mortar strength. Mix thoroughly.

5 Lay a bed of mortar with the trowel, then, buttering the end of one brick, lay it in the mortar against the existing work. Tap it down with the handle of the trowel and along until it lines up with the existing bricks. The vertical joint should be around 10 mm. Check the brick for level. When it's correct, cut off any excess mortar with the trowel. This excess mortar can be returned to the main lot and re-used).

6 Lay another bed and repeat the procedure until all the bricks are laid.

7 While the mortar is still semi-soft, rake or iron the joint. Try to remove any excess mortar from the face of the bricks by scraping and brushing. Don't forget to clean your trowel and shovel thoroughly when you're finished!

8 Leave the new brickwork to cure for a week or more and then, if necessary, remove any stubborn stains by brushing on muriatic acid (a diluted mixture of hydrochloric acid and water). Wear gloves and old, protective clothes. When clean, thoroughly hose the section off.

A gap in a wall where a brick has come loose.

Clean the old mortar off the loose and the bonded bricks.

Replace half bricks with whole bricks wherever possible.

It is important to establish a level bottom line.

Try one of the replacement bricks for size, allowing for mortar.

Apply a generous layer of mortar to the joints and the new brick.

Insert new brick, taking care not to disturb the mortar.

Cut small sections of brick by tapping with the comb chisel or bolster.

Make the top of the split brick level with other bricks; adjust mortar.

The last brick is the hardest — you may need to cut the corners.

Apply final layer of mortar, filling evenly down each side.

While the mortar is semi-soft, iron or rake the joint.

Cutting Down Doors

Often because of poor hanging, swelling in the door, or new carpet, you'll find the door scrubbing the pile off the berber or carving a semi-circular hole in the floorboards. The solution is easy. Shorten the door!

Measure the amount you want to take off the bottom of the door.

Wedge the top of the door and if the amount is small, plane it off.

TOOLS

You'll need: a screwdriver, a plane (for taking off amounts up to 5 mm or for making the bottom of the door smooth), a panel saw (for removing amounts over 5 mm), some glue in case you have to glue the bottom rail back in (only for hollow core doors), a pencil and rule or tape.

PROCEDURE

1 Decide on how much you want to take off the bottom of the door. A clearance of 10 mm above the floor surface is usual but in draughty situations you may want to have less (but don't go below 5 mm). With the door closed, measure the required clearance on both edges of the door and mark clearly.

2 Open the door completely and examine the screws. If the slots are filled with paint, scrape it out with a nail or small screwdriver.

3 Using the correct sized screwdriver (the tip fits neatly in the slot and is the same width as the screw or slightly smaller) undo the screws. Put them in a safe place.

4 Lay the door on a pair of stools or a blanket-covered table and draw a straight line between the two marks. Transfer these marks to the other side of the door.

5 If planing the clearance, wedge the top of the door into the corner of a room to hold it steady (a blanket around it will save any damage) and place two or three thick books under the edge of the door. Then take your sharp plane and begin planing the bottom of the door. Do not plane right through otherwise you may chip the edge of the door. Turn the door over and plane from the other edge, again not running right through. Stop when you reach the line; then, sighting along the bottom to check it is straight, put a small chamfer (bevel) on both edges of the bottom to make a neat finish.

6 Using a block or some thin books, lift the door until the hinges line up with the gains in the jamb, and then replace the screws. Touch up the screw heads with some matching paint.

7 If there is too much to plane off, you will have to rip the waste off with a saw. Using a trimming knife and straight edge, cut through the ply or timber on the back of the door to a depth of at least 1.0 mm. Then when you start to rip the timber will not splinter off on the far side.

8 Lay the door on its back and cut it through keeping just a fraction away from the line. Be careful when you get near the finish that the waste piece does not split off.

9 If the door is a hollow core door and you have had to cut a fair amount off you may find that the whole bottom rail is cut out. In this case, peel the veneer off the offcut with a chisel, plane it smooth (being careful you don't make it smaller) then glue it back in, using plenty of glue. Some heavy objects will substitute for a clamp to ensure a tight joint. Alternatively nail through the face of the door with panel pins, punch, then allow to dry.

10 Set up the door ready for planing, make the bottom smooth, then chamfer the edges, putty the holes and paint all bare surfaces. Painting the bottom is essential because bare timber absorbs moisture from the air. If the rest of the door is sealed and the bottom isn't, you get unequal expansion which can cause buckling, to say nothing of possible delamination. Rehang the door, following the procedure in step 6.

If sawing, mark the line to be cut with a trimming knife to reduce splintering.

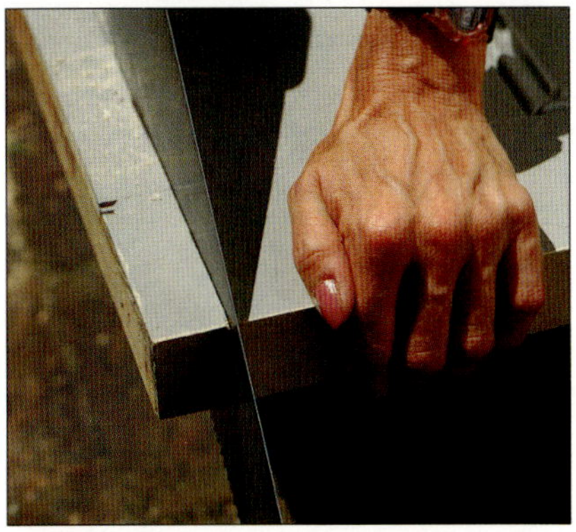

Lay the door on its back and cut it through.

With a hollow core door you may find that the bottom rail is cut out.

Glue the bottom rail back in, using plenty of glue.

Fixing a Springy Floor

The problem of a springy floor can be caused by a bearer twisting or curling off its support. Another reason might be a pier has settled and left the bearer stranded in mid-air. Either way the result is a little like a trampoline — the floor bounces when you walk on it!

To solve the problem get under the house and, with a torch, find what is causing it. To establish whether it is a bowed bearer or sunken pier, simply sight along the bearer. If it looks like the Sydney Harbour Bridge then follow the first procedure.

Underfloor Maintenance

While you're under the house check for white ant trails up the foundation walls. These pesky termites build mud tunnels up the foundations walls and then dine on your timber framing (unless it has been preserved). If you find any evidence, call in a pest exterminator to establish the extent of the damage, if any, and have the ground sprayed with a suitable pesticide.

While you're there, remove any old timber that might be lying around to attract white ants. Also look for damp patches that might be caused by leaking plumbing or surface drainage running under your house. Check for rotting in floor timbers also.

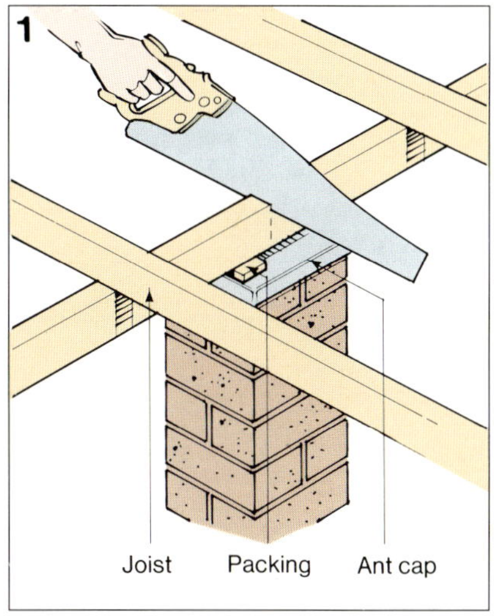

Saw through the bearer until it sits hard down on the pier.

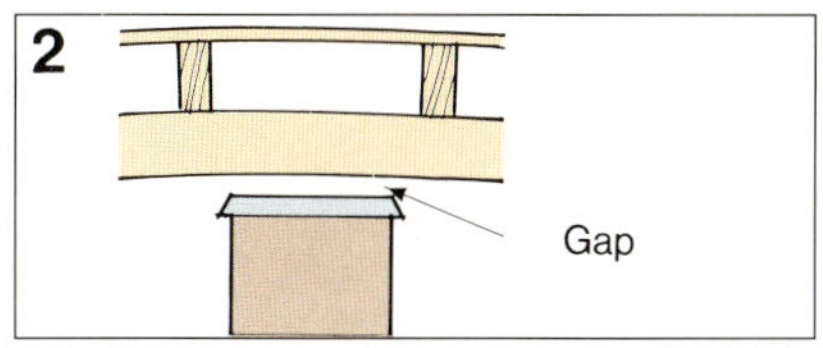

Springy floor resulting from bowed bearer.

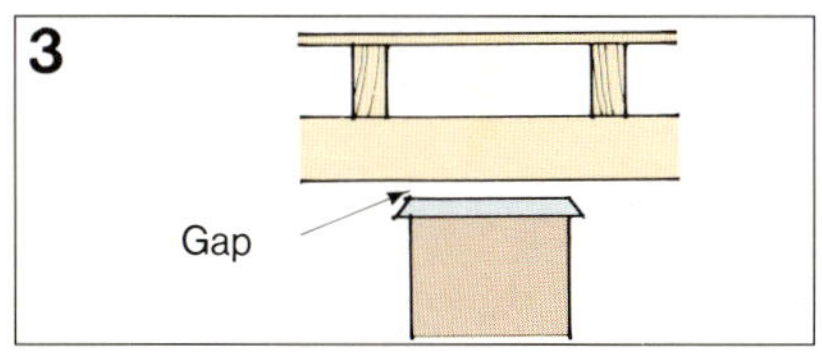

Springy floor resulting from sunken pier.

PROCEDURE FOR BOWED BEARER

You'll need a lead light, some packing, and a handsaw. Where the bearer has warped above the pier, temporarily pack it with some fibrous cement offcuts or thin timber shims so it is solid, but remember: you have to get them out again! Then cut the bearer part-way through over the pier with a handsaw. It's an awkward thing to do, but patience will eventually reward you.

Then, using a chisel or pinch bar, lever the bearer up, remove the packing and see if it sits down. If it doesn't, repack it and cut through the bearer even further until it sits hard down on the pier.

If you're not a perfectionist and you don't care if the floor has a camber in it, you could cheat and just pack the bearer tightly!

PROCEDURE FOR SUNKEN PIER

If the pier has sunk down below the bearer, leaving a space, get a piece of fibre cement or other suitable packing material such as metal damp proofing. It must be something that won't rot. Then drive it in tight under the bearer until there is no movement.

Patching Ceramic Floor Tiles

Ever had an annoying spot where you wish the floor tiler had gone a little further? Or moved a door opening and now the tiling doesn't quite go under the door? Putting in a few extra tiles is not difficult.

Fix the screed in position and mark the tiles.

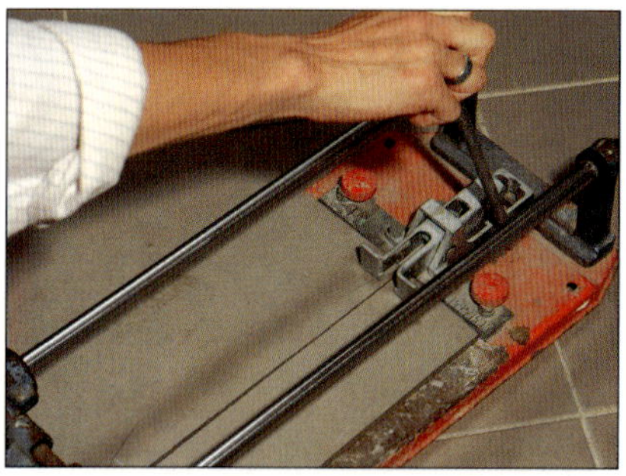

Use a tile cutter to score the surface of the tiles.

Apply the tile bed with a trowel, leaving it slightly full.

Lay the tiles in place and carefully tap them down.

TOOLS AND MATERIALS

You'll need a tile cutter, small trowel or spreader, a Carborundum stone (for smoothing off the rough edges of cut tiles), a scrap piece of timber (screed) to support the thick bed until it dries (this may have to be temporarily nailed to plugs in the brickwork), a straight edge (to check the new tiling lines up with the old), and a rule and pencil.

You'll also need sufficient tiles to cover the area (allow some extras in case of breakages or problems with cutting). For thin bed joints (up to 3 mm) use an adhesive. For thick bed joints (up to 25 mm) use a cement and sand mix which has some PVA type glue in it (Bondcrete or Semstick, etc.) to increase adhesion.

Because of the number of types and brands of adhesives on the market you would be well advised to consult a few reputable tile suppliers and ask their advice about your particular situation. If using thin bed adhesives, get some grout as well!

PROCEDURE

1 Prepare the subsurface so it is perfectly clean, firm and dry. Roughening it will assist adhesion.

2 Fix the screed (which could be lightly oiled to make sure it doesn't stick to the mortar) in position either by tacking to a timber floor or jamb or, as shown, by drilling the brickwork with a masonry drill and plugging the hole with timber plugs (these plugs can later be drilled out, filled and touched up with paint). If you're butting against a carpet, a brass strip will provide the most attractive finish.

3 Mark the tiles, then, using the tile cutter, score the surface heavily with the cutter. Place a match under the cut and press down. Use the stone to make the edges smooth. A professional tile cutting machine which can be hired makes it easy.

4 Mix up the tile bed to a paste-like consistency and apply, leaving it slightly full.

5 Lay the tiles in place and carefully tap them down with a wooden block or the handle of a hammer until they are level with the existing floor. If there is too much mortar, scrape it out because if you hit the tiles too hard they may crack!

6 Using the straight edge, make sure the tiles line up with the existing floor and adjust as necessary.

7 Wipe off all excess mortar, fill then smooth the joints, and allow to dry fully. Then carefully remove the screed.

Don't walk on the retiled area for at least three days to allow the mortar time to cure.

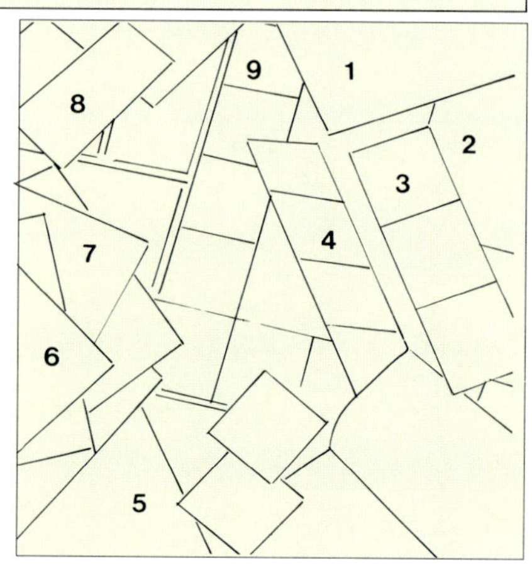

Ceramic floor tiles
1. Federation-style pattern
2. Unglazed terracotta
3. Small unglazed terracotta
4. Glazed co-ordinates for edging
5. Mosaic tiles
6. Imitation terracotta
7. Selection of printed tiles
8. Non-slip stair edge
9. Square low-sheen glaze

Replacing a Rusty Arch Bar

An arch bar, for the uninitiated, is a flat piece of mild steel which bridges across a small window or door opening in a brick wall to support the brickwork above (for larger spans, angle irons are used). Unless the arch bar has been hot-dip galvanised, there is a high chance of rust attacking the metal, especially in coastal areas where there is salt in the air.

Unfortunately, rusting metal expands, creating great pressure. The problem is usually evidenced by a gradually increasing crack in the brick joint on either side of the window opening.

If the opening is small (not more than approximately one metre) and accessible, you could try replacing the bar yourself. Angle irons, because of their size and the amount of brickwork above them, would usually require the services of a licensed builder.

An old steel arch bar which has rusted.

Drill a series of holes in the joint under the top brick.

Use a plugging chisel to loosen the top bricks.

Remove the top brick on either side of the brick reveal.

Thoroughly wet the tops of the reveal and the two bricks.

Tap the new arch bar into position.

Lay a generous bed joint where the reveal bricks will sit.

TOOLS AND MATERIALS

You'll need an electric drill and 6 mm masonry bit (or a plugging chisel), hammer, cold chisel, saw, trowel, shovel, and brick jointing tool.

Order a hot-dip galvanised arch bar the same size as the existing one. Some mortar sand, cement (and oxide if the brick joints are coloured) and a spot of lime will make the mortar to relay the bricks. A piece of scrap timber to temporarily prop up the brickwork in the centre of the opening is a good idea.

PROCEDURE

1 First, carefully examine the bricks over the opening. If they are loose or in a soft lime mortar, it would be better to remove and relay them otherwise they could fall on you. If they are solid and the existing mortar is high in cement (if so, it'll be difficult to scratch out with a nail), they should support themselves during the changeover with the help of the prop.

2 Cut the temporary prop between the floor or sill and the brickwork (not the arch bar) and tap into place in the middle.

3 With the masonry bit (or plugging chisel), drill a series of holes in the brick joint under the top brick on either side of the brick reveal. Then drill out the vertical joint. Carefully remove each brick. Tap the arch bar loose and withdraw.

4 After cleaning any lumps of mortar off the bricks, thoroughly wet the tops of the reveal and the two bricks. Put the new arch bar in position (or wedge it up with another prop). Then mix up the mortar (proportions of 6 of sand and one each of lime and cement are suitable). Lay a generous bed joint where the reveal bricks will sit. Butter some mortar on the ends of the reveal bricks and push them into place (see previous topic). Make sure they are in line with the existing bricks (otherwise the crack won't close up).

5 Fill any holes (but not the cracks) and then use your trowel to cut off the excess mortar. Leave the joint until the mortar is semi-hard, then finish to suit the existing work (ironed, raked, etc.). Clean off any stains and leave the prop for 24 hours, until the mortar has cured sufficiently to take any weight. The cracks should close up when you take the prop out (assuming you haven't left any dags of mortar on top of the bricks). If they don't, mix up some more mortar and fill them.

6 Next paint the arch bar to increase its anti-rust properties. To do this, first wipe it carefully with mineral turpentine, then apply a galvanised iron primer and, when dry, finish off with two coats of suitable exterior grade paint.

Tap the old arch bar loose and take it out.

Finish the semi-dry mortar with an iron or rake.

The new arch bar in place after completing the work.

Hiding Wiring with Timber Conduits

After a house or unit is finished and the occupants move in, it often becomes apparent there are insufficient power points or lights — in fact, one might almost say this is a law of nature!

However, putting in extra outlets sometimes leaves ugly exposed wiring running part-way up walls or across ceilings (either because it's too expensive or difficult to run it down cavities, under floors, or fit it behind architraves). Why not camouflage it?

One way to hide the wiring is to cover it with a small timber section that has a groove in the back for the wiring to fit into. The section may then be painted in with the wall, made into a feature by painting it another colour, or wallpapered over.

If the wiring runs part-way up a wall you should consider running the section the full height of the wall. That looks much better than stopping it half way. If it is a horizontal run, why not make a feature of it and put the wiring at chair rail or picture rail height and run the grooved section right around the room? On ceilings, run it from cornice to cornice.

The groove in the timber can be made two ways:

- by buying a solid section and running a groove in it with a router, or
- by building up the grooved section from three separate pieces.

ROUTER SAFETY HINTS

- Unplug the router while making any adjustments.
- Remember to KEEP BOTH YOUR HANDS ON THE ROUTER.
- Work from left to right (because the bit revolves in a clockwise direction).
- Wear safety glasses to protect your eyes.
- Make sure the cutter and the fence are secure.
- Start the machine with the cutter clear of the timber.

The tools and timber needed for making timber conduits.

Insert the cutter in the router and adjust to the right depth.

Make sure the cutter and guide are fixed tightly.

Clamp the timber and fix the router in position.

Rout out the groove, holding the router with both hands.

Check the grooved timber for correct fit.

Fix the timber in position and punch nails.

MATERIALS IF YOU ARE ROUTING

You'll require a dressed timber section that is thick enough to be safely grooved to hold the wire (allow for at least 2 mm clearance around the wire) and of sufficient width so that when fixing it, you won't nail through the wiring (but not too wide or it becomes too obvious).

MATERIALS IF YOU ARE BUILDING UP

Buy one length of 50 × 13 mm dressed batten and two lengths of 13 × 13 mm dressed strip. Some wood glue and a few 18 mm brads will make up the section.

TOOLS AND FIXING MATERIALS

For either option, you'll also require 38 mm nails if fixing through gypsum plaster into timber studs, ceiling joists or battens. If there is no timber to fix to, you may have to consider gluing the batten to the wall or ceiling with epoxy glue or contact glue. Hold the batten in place with masking tape until the glue dries. If fastening to masonry walls, you'll need plugs and a masonry drill. Whatever type of wall you have, you will need putty and paint.

If using solid timber, you'll need an electric router with fence and a suitable cutter. This can be hired from most hire outlets but make sure you tell them what size groove you want to cut and get them to show you how to set up the fence and adjust the depth of cut.

A hammer, nail punch, plane, masonry bit and electric drill (for plugs), pencil and rule, and sandpaper will also be required.

PROCEDURE

A. If ROUTING, mark out the desired width of the groove and then set the router up so the cutter extends to the right depth. If it's a deep groove it may be better to take two or three shallow bites at it.

Try the router out on a scrap piece of timber first but make sure the piece is securely held by temporarily nailing it to a bench or stool so it can't move (use a couple of 38 mm nails). If it's correct, remove the scrap piece, temporarily secure the full length timber section in position and run the groove.

B. If MAKING THE BUILT-UP SECTION, lay the two 13 x 13 mm dressed strips side by side, and spread a generous layer of glue on an edge of each one. Using the brads, nail the 50 x 13 mm dressed battens on top of them, keeping them flush with the outside edge. When the glue is dry, lightly sand the section and take off the sharp corners.

FIXING PROCEDURE

1 Cut the grooved batten to length and try it over the wire. Adjust the groove if necessary. You may find it easier to fit if the wire clips are removed. Use tape to hold the wire in place. Check also that the back of the section fits neatly against the wall surface on both sides. Plane it if necessary.

2 Fix the batten in position watching you don't nail through the wire! Punch the nails, fill the holes, then apply a suitable finish. Alternatively, glue it on.

If you still consider the camouflage too obtrusive, hang a large picture on the batten or allow a climbing vine to grow up it!

Glazing

Getting broken glass replaced in timber windows can be a real pain! It's expensive too if your insurance doesn't cover it. Why not do it yourself? Replacing the glass in a small accessible frame can be easy if you follow these steps. Removing a sash from the frame will make the job easier. But remember, glass cuts like a surgical knife, so be careful!

Preparation

The first thing to do is to hack out the old facing putty. Use your second-best chisel and a hammer. Choose a day when your patience is good because, if the window is old, you will probably find that the putty has gone hard and will be stuck like glue to the rebate. Care is required or you'll damage the frame.

Next remove the headless nails (sprigs) with a pair of pliers, and then carefully remove the old back putty, again taking care you don't damage the frame.

Tap out the remaining glass and put it in an old ice-cream container. Don't just put it in a plastic garbage bag — it's dangerous.

Liberally paint the rebate with oil-based primer otherwise the timber will suck the oil out of the putty causing it to crack and fall out. Allow to dry overnight. Some plastic taped over the opening will stop rain and wind if necessary.

Carefully hack out the old facing putty.

Pull out the old sprigs with a pair of pliers.

Use a paint scraper to remove the back putty.

TOOLS AND MATERIALS

With a steel tape or folding rule, measure the exact size of the opening, then go to your hardware store or nearest glass supplier, give them the sizes and tell them where the glass is to be used. They will make the necessary allowances for clearance (2 mm all around) and give you the correct weight (thickness) and type of glass (some situations require safety glass). Buy also some glazing putty, some new sprigs, and a putty knife. It is best to carry the glass on its edge.

PROCEDURE

1 Take a handful of putty and keep squeezing it until it grows soft. Add linseed oil if it's a bit old. Squeeze the dough-like putty around the back of the rebate.

2 Carefully pick up the glass and press it into place (but not in the centre) making sure you maintain an even clearance around the perimeter. Use a couple of matches at the bottom as a spacer. There should be at least a 2 mm thickness of putty at the back.

3 Tap in some sprigs (say every 250 mm) sliding a small hammer or large chisel gently across the face of the glass.

4 Again softening some putty, press it liberally along the front of the rebate using your thumb or putty knife.

5 Using the putty knife, smooth off the facing putty making the bevel approximately the same as on the other windows (that is, in line with the inside of the rebate). Work from the corners into the centre. The bevel gives a neat finish and helps the rain to run off.

6 Using the putty knife, scrape or cut off excess putty from the outside and inside and clean off all marks with a rag dipped in methylated spirits. Leave to cure for a week or so before painting. Make sure you eventually paint it otherwise it will dry out and crack. This could allow water to get into the timber, potentially leading to rotting.

Steel windows can be glazed similarly, providing you cut out any rust and treat the bare metal with metal primer (you'll find clips are used instead of sprigs). However, never use wood putty on metal windows — they need special metal putty.

Aluminium windows, unfortunately, generally require professional attention.

Repairing Windows

Gently press the new sheet of glass into place.

Press putty liberally into the front of the rebate.

Smooth off the putty with the putty knife.

A window generally consists of a fixed frame to which lighter units called sashes are fitted. These sashes hold the glass and move in a variety of directions (sliding, outward opening, etc.). Windows are generally made from timber, aluminium or steel.

The major problems associated with windows are:

- broken glass (see Glazing);
- rotting or rusting of the frame or sash (see Repairing Rotting Door Frames);
- the sashes become difficult or impossible to open. It is this factor that we will look at.

Timber Casement Sashes

These sashes open outwards on hinges (like doors) or by the use of friction stays. If the sashes are difficult to open it will usually be for one of the reasons given below:

Continuous painting has closed the clearance gap. If this has happened, treat the same as for Sticking Doors.

Water has penetrated into the joints because of cracked glazing putty or peeling paint and the glue has given way allowing the sash to sag. The only effective way to correct this problem is to take the sash out of the frame, tap the joints apart and, after cleaning off the old glue, reglue them with a waterproof glue such as epoxy.

Unfortunately you'll require a sash cramp to pull the joints tight, although you can also do it by nailing a series of blocks to a bench or old table and using wedges. Check that the frame is square by making the diagonals the same.

When dry, carefully repaint the joint and surrounding area with primer, undercoat and finishing coats and reputty where necessary.

The screws may have also pulled loose. The holes should be replugged the same way as for loose catches.

Friction stays that are difficult to operate require lubrication. Clean any grit or dirt out of the fitting with turps, then use Vaseline or one of the dry lubricants obtainable from your petrol station to lessen friction. Some candle wax will do in an emergency.

If rust has damaged the stay it should be replaced. Make sure you get two of a similar size.

Horizontal Sliding Sashes

These may be of timber or metal and run on a metal track using either nylon or roller bearings. If they are sticking, clear away any dirt that has built up in the track, then re-lubricate the bearings with grease or graphite.

If this doesn't work, check whether the top of the window frame is rubbing on the top of the sash. If this is happening then some settlement has taken place (quite normal). With a timber sash, you can remove the beading or trim which holds it in place, then lift the sash out and plane the top of it until it has 2–3 mm clearance.

Alternatively, locate the area of deflection and drive a nail up through the timber lining into the window head to try to pull the top of the window frame upwards.

If neither of these solutions works, call in a builder to help you with the problem.

Vertical Sliding Windows

The two most common ways to make these windows work are spiral balances or weights and cords. In the case of a spiral balance that is weak, undo the bottom clasp and, turn the clasp several times to the left. That should retighten the spring. Screw the clasp back on and see if it works.

If the spring is broken, replace the balance but make sure you get two (if one's gone, it's likely the other one won't be far away). They must be the same size or they may not support the weight of the sash.

Replacing broken or badly rotted cords in wooden box frame windows is a fairly tricky job. Check first in your piggy bank to see if there isn't enough money to pay a carpenter to do it (assuming you can find one who is willing and knows what to do!).

Vertical sash window sometimes become difficult to open.

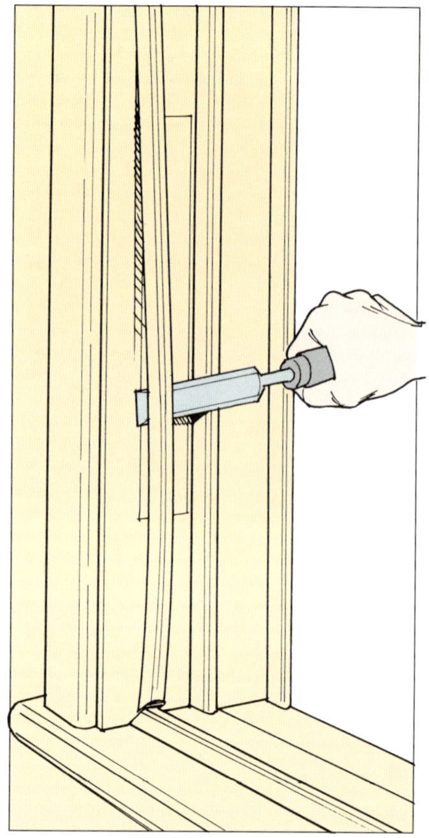

2. Insert a chisel under the middle of the side stop bead.

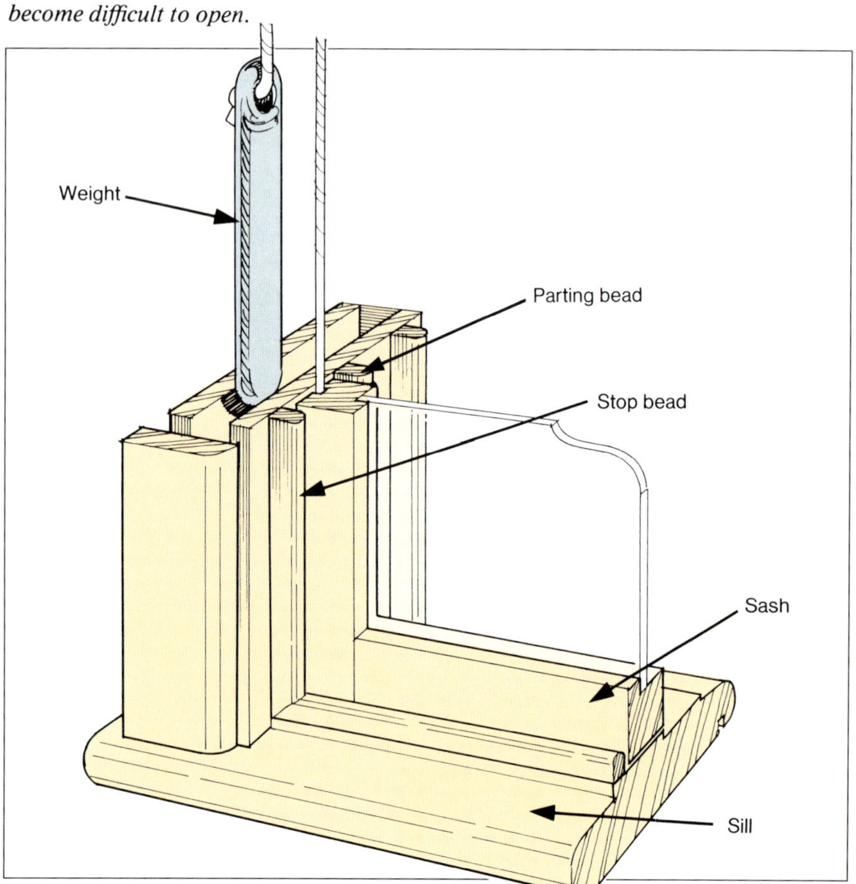

1. Section showing the parts of a double-hung sash window.

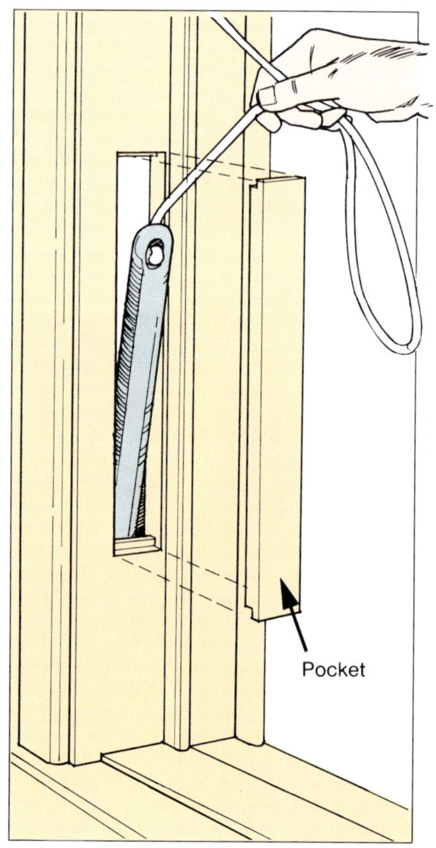

3. Lever out the pocket and retrieve the sash weight.

Replacing Sash Cords

TOOLS AND MATERIALS

You'll need an old chisel, hammer, paint scraper, a few 38 mm nails, a handful of 25 mm galvanised clouts and a roll of sash cord. A roll might seem too much but, if one cord is broken, others will surely follow.

PROCEDURE

1 First study Diagram 1 and identify all the parts on your window. Then carefully insert a chisel under the middle of the side stop bead and, tapping it under with the hammer, begin to lever it off. With a pencil, clearly mark where it goes; then repeat for the other side.

2 Next, cut the bottom sash cords, if any, with a trimming knife and carefully lower the weights down inside the box. Then remove the bottom sash (work the chisel or screwdriver into the joint if it is stuck because of built-up paint).

3 The parting beads, which fit into a groove in the pulley stile, have to come out next. Insert a fine chisel or screwdriver and carefully prise them out (if they or the stop beads break, you may have to make a quick trip to the timber yard to find a replacement — make sure you take a broken piece with you so you can match it). Label them also to make sure they go back in the same place.

4 Lower the top sash, cut the top cords, and remove the top sash. Remove the nails and offcuts of cord from the sash stiles. Scrape or plane away any paint build-up so the sash will slide easily.

5 Next, lever out the pockets with a chisel or screwdriver and retrieve the sash weights. Mark where they belong. If one is bigger than the other, the larger one belongs with the bottom sash (assuming they are both the same glass size) because it has a wider and therefore heavier bottom rail.

6 Make a 'mouse' to help thread the sash cord. This is achieved by attaching a small piece of sheet lead (a thin sinker could also work) to a 1.5 metre length of string. Fix the other end of the string to the end of the new sash cord. Push the mouse through the top pulley hole and allow it to fall to the bottom of the pocket. Retrieve it, then pull the cord through.

7 Fix the top weight to the end of the cord using a figure-of-eight knot, and then push the weight back into the box. Put the top sash in the outside channel and let it rest on the sill. Then pull the cord tight until the weight bumps up against the pulley. Lower it a fraction, then tack a 38 mm nail through the cord 150 mm below the pulley (to hold the weight up).

8 Swivel the sash outwards and nail the cord into the groove in the edge of the sash using the clouts. Four should suffice. Repeat for the other side; then remove the 38 mm nails.

9 Then repeat the procedure for the bottom sash but watch that you lower the cord approximately 100 mm below the pulley before you tack it in place (this stops the weights hitting on the pulley). Then replace the pockets, parting beads and stop beads in that order.

10 Check that the sashes slide before you nail the stop bead off.

If everything works properly, you can have the rest of the day off. We've earned it. If there are other cords to replace, don't leave it too long or you might forget how it's done.

4. Thread the new sash cord with the help of a 'mouse'.

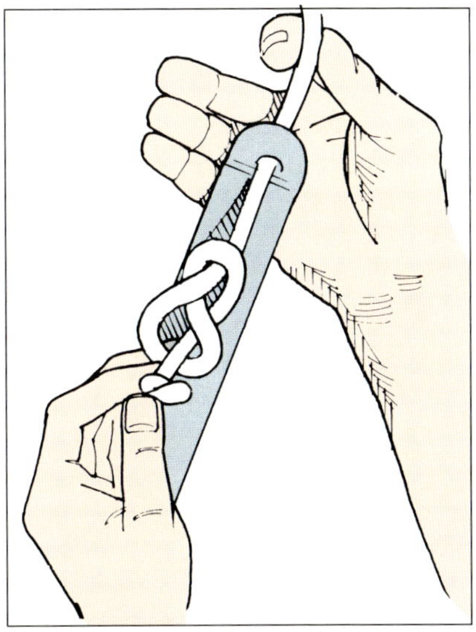

5. Fix the weight to the end of the cord with a figure-of-eight knot.

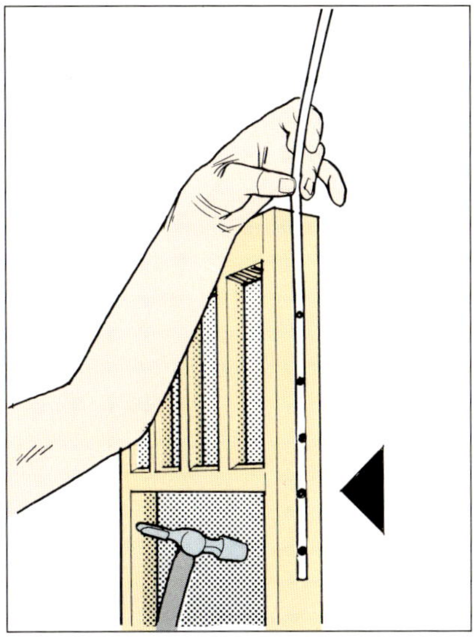

6. Nail the cord into the groove in the edge of the sash.

Removing and Replacing Wallpaper

Wallpapering is a messy job that brings most people unstuck. But it needn't!

Before you begin, remember, what looks attractive in a small piece can look disastrous in large areas. It is helpful if the book you choose the paper from has photographs of rooms as well as small samples of the actual paper.

The type of paper you select (vinyl, textile, etc.) should be governed by the room use. Areas that are to be subjected to water, steam or continual cleaning require a washable surface. Various different types of wallpaper are illustrated on page 94.

If you have never hung wallpaper before, choose a small room to start with. A child's bedroom is ideal for the beginner.

You can hire steaming equipment to remove old paper.

Work down the wall in consecutive strips.

Mark a vertical starting line with a level or plumb line.

Cut measured lengths of paper, always allowing extra.

Pull length of prepasted paper through water trough.

Fold each end to the middle of the drop.

Surface Preparation

It's best to remove all old wallpaper and glue. This can be done by soaking it in hot water that has detergent or stripping solution in it. A better method involves steaming it off (equipment to do this can be hired). Well-bonded, non-vinyl, non-textured paper can be papered over (ask your supplier for advice).

If stripping, score the surface of the previously painted wallpaper with a wire brush or coarse sandpaper to assist water penetration. On plasterboard surfaces make sure you don't overwet the paper or you may lift the lining paper on the plaster. This is not a problem if the plasterboard has been properly painted in the first place.

When the wallpaper is properly dampened, begin to scrape it off with a wide stripping knife, being careful you don't damage the wall surface. When the wallpaper is removed, fill all holes and paint any bare patches with an oil-based sealer.

New plasterboard and cement render must be properly cured before sealing. Previously painted surfaces must be free of flaking paint, totally clean (use sugar soap) and lightly sandpapered. All cracks must be filled and sanded. Any mould must be removed and the wall treated with an anti-mould solution.

Size the walls to slow down the adhesive setting time. This gives you a chance to position the paper properly before it sticks!

Apply the first drop to the wall against the marked line.

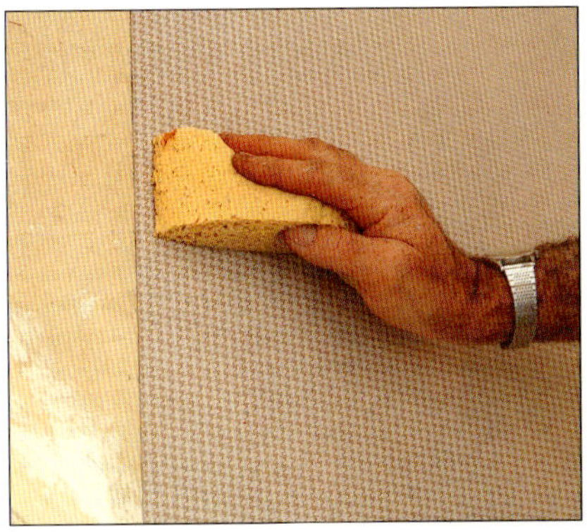

Smooth paper from top to bottom with a damp sponge.

Trim the top edges using a metal edge as a guide.

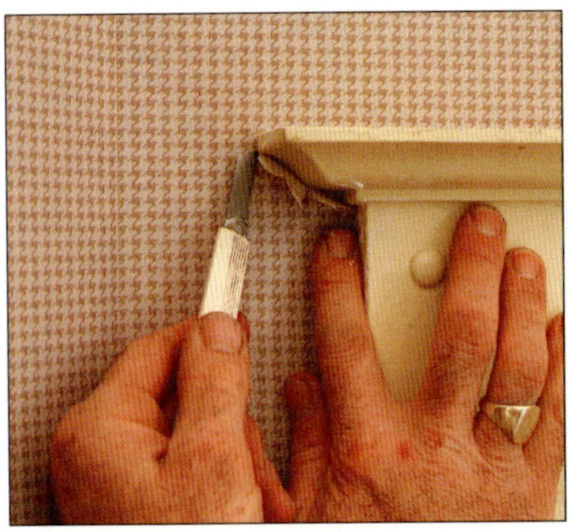

Trim around difficult edges with a knife or scissors.

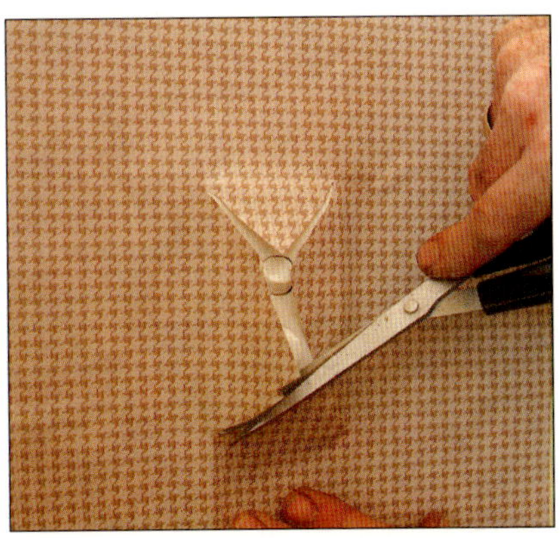

Cut paper diagonally to corners over light switch.

Hanging Wallpaper

TOOLS AND MATERIALS

Carefully measure the width and height of each wall and draw a small sketch of each. Make a note of any large windows, doors, and the type and condition of the wall finish. From your drawings the supplier will calculate the number of rolls you'll need and advise on the surface preparation, the paste required (though most wallpaper is now pre-pasted) and whether you'll need to put up lining paper first (if so, hang it horizontally).

If using a non-pasted paper, a kitchen table or an old door makes a good pasting table while a 100–200 mm paint brush can be used for pasting. A water trough is almost essential for pre-pasted papers. A broad hanging brush or smoother helps to work out any bubbles. Scissors should be as large as possible and a trimming knife is handy for fitting the paper in awkward places.

A sponge, bucket, rule and pencil, spirit level or string with weight attached, drop sheet and stepladder complete the essential equipment.

PROCEDURE

1 Select a day when you're at peace with the world. Cut the paper into full lengths allowing 100–150 mm waste. Match the pattern on each strip as you go and number each one.

2 To ensure the sheets are perfectly vertical, make a plumb line. Use a spirit level or tie a heavy nut or piece of lead to a length of string. Tape it to the ceiling where required, then, when the line is still, mark it in several places with a pencil. Then remove the line and simply join the marks with a straight edge to achieve a perfect starting point.

3 Begin next to a window and continue right around the room. Hanging away from a strong light will help to disguise the joins and avoid glare. If the window is not exactly plumb and straight, trim the first sheet around it until the other edge hangs vertically.

4 If you're pasting, start at one end. Do the middle first, then the edges. Fold the end in towards the centre while you do the other half. Fold similarly, then carry the folded strip to the window and, getting up the ladder, release the top half. Smooth into position with the hanging brush making sure the top overlaps the cornice 40–50 mm. Work from the centre out to avoid trapping air bubbles. Then release the bottom half. Don't overwork thin paper as it may tear.

For pre-pasted paper, place the trough against the wall, roll the paper with the pattern inside, then place in the water. Slowly draw the length past the bar and hang.

5 Next run the back edge of the scissors along the skirting board and ceiling (treat architraves similarly), then peel the paper back far enough to enable you to cut it to length. Clean all excess glue off then brush the paper back into position.

Alternatively, cut it in position using the smoother to steady the paper while cutting with a sharp trimming knife. Check for air bubbles and creases by looking along the sheet towards the light and brush them out.

6 Corners are rarely plumb or straight so cut the last strip so it goes around the corner just 15 mm. Paste into position. Then use the offcut to return along the next wall, overlapping it on top of the 15 mm until the far edge is vertical (but only if the pattern allows it). Paste into position and continue. On all external corners allow 25 mm overlap also. Paper around window reveals first.

7 With light switches and power points, first switch the power off at the meter box. Hang the paper and then, from the centre of the fitting, cut four diagonals to the corners. Trim as for cornices. You've done it! I knew you could.

ROCK

Moving a Cupboard

Ever had the feeling that your kitchen's appearance would be greatly improved if the top cupboards were located somewhere else? Why not move them? It's not such a difficult job and the end result could be brilliant, to say nothing of a potential increase in kitchen efficiency.

Cupboards are normally fixed to the wall by screws. In the case of timber frame construction, the screws usually go into studs. With masonry construction the wall is drilled and plugged to provide solid fixing. All that has to be done, therefore, is to undo the screws, remove the cupboard or cupboards, and refix the unit in the more favoured position (but first carefully measure the area to make sure it will fit).

Remember also to check with your local authorities as to how many millimetres you should keep above a stove (and a refrigerator) should they be involved. And above all, when nailing or screwing, watch you don't hit any electrical wiring or plumbing!

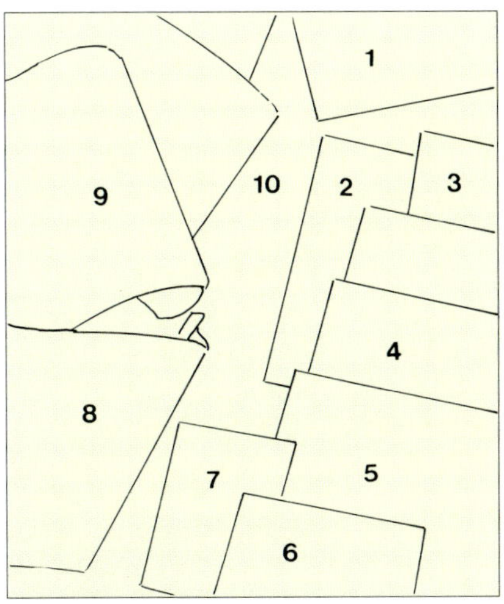

Wallcoverings
1. *Wall cork*
2. *Pastel print paper*
3. *Synthetic grass-like wallcovering*
4. *Pure linen weave, paper backing*
5. *Rag roll print*
6. *Suede-like wall covering*
7. *Moiré textured wall covering*
8. *Art Nouveau border*
9. *Selection of borders*
10. *Heavy textured vinyl*

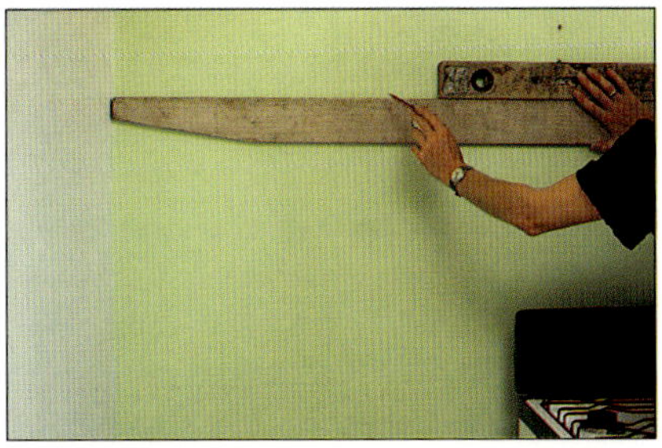

Mark the new position of the cupboard, using a level.

With cupboard held in new position, punch through screw holes.

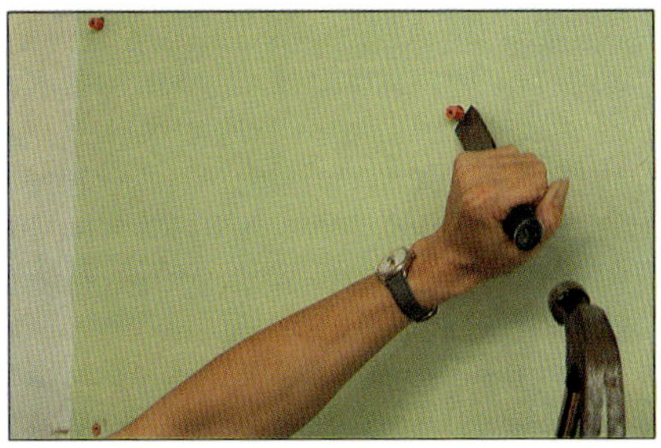

Plug walls and cut off excess plugs with a chisel.

With a friend's help screw the cupboard in the new position.

TOOLS AND MATERIALS

Buy new screws (unless you can get the old ones out without damaging the heads) and plugs if necessary. You'll need a hefty screwdriver (ratchet if possible) that neatly fits the screw heads, a hand or electric drill plus drill bits (include a tungsten-tipped masonry bit if drilling brickwork), a tape and pencil, level, hammer, 50 mm nails, and half a kilogram of fortitude.

PROCEDURE

1 Remove the contents of the cupboard and then clear the screw heads of any paint with, say, a nail file or steel skewer.

2 Look to see whether the top cupboard is a single unit or several units fixed together. If in sections, undo the side fastenings (but check each unit is secured to the wall).

3 To support the cupboard, enlist the aid of a sympathetic and robust friend or build two pillars of support under each end using say books or paint tins. Then undo the screws and remove the cupboard (if you're by yourself and it's too heavy, it may pay to remove the cupboard doors to make the unit lighter).

4 Mark the position where the bottom of the cupboard will go, using the tape. Level this line across the wall (if you haven't got a level, you could measure off the floor cupboards).

5 With the help of a friend place the cupboard in the new location. Use a nail punch or narrow screwdriver to mark the existing screw holes on the wall; then remove the cupboard. Drill and plug the holes (make sure they're at least 3 mm deeper than the amount the driven screw will project past the cupboard), and then fix the cupboard in place.

For timber frame walls you can locate the stud positions by tapping the wall while listening for a solid sound. Drive in a nail to verify solid fixing. Mark these stud positions (usually at 450 or 600 mm centres) *below* the level line, then, with the cupboard in place, drill new screw holes in the back of the cupboard opposite these positions and rescrew the unit to the wall.

Relaying a Concrete Path

Concrete paths, because of bad proportioning or mixing, inadequate reinforcing, or incorrect jointing between slabs or poor foundations, can crack. Taking up the old concrete and laying a new path is not very difficult but it is not recommended for anyone with a bad back!

Removing the Old Concrete

First, break up the old concrete. The best hand tool for this is the sledge hammer. If there is a hire outlet nearby, an electric Kanga makes the job easier. Before you begin, check if the path has expansion joints. If it has, these will provide a convenient spot to join the old with the new.

If it hasn't, then you may have to cut through the path at both ends of the cracked section with an electric saw that has an abrasive disc in it, one suitable for cutting concrete (read the section on electric tools). While doing this make sure you wear goggles. Take two or three bites rather than try to cut right through the slab in one go. This will lessen the chance of the blade twisting and shattering.

Begin to break up the slab into pieces that are small enough to carry. When removing the waste, remember to lift with your legs, not your back!

Once the old concrete has been disposed of, remove weeds and fill any low spots with gravel or chips of concrete. A heavy roller, which can be hired, could also help to consolidate the foundation.

For various reasons, a concrete path can develop cracks.

TOOLS AND MATERIALS

You'll need a lump hammer to drive the pegs, a shovel for mixing and spreading the concrete, hacksaw to cut the mesh, a straight edge for levelling the concrete and a wooden float for finishing.

You'll need sufficient concrete for the job. The volume can be established by multiplying the length in metres by the width in metres by 0.075. This will allow for a path 75 mm thick. If it's a drive, which should be 100 mm thick and well reinforced with steel mesh, multiply by 0.100. Refer to Materials for calculating the amount of dry material per cubic metre. Consider using ready-mix if you don't have or can't hire a concrete mixer. Small areas can be done in a wheelbarrow using dry-mix.

You'll also need two screeds 75 x 25 mm long enough to cover the length of the new path plus sufficient hardwood pegs to hold them in place. A handful of 50 mm nails, light reinforcing mesh, and some strips of 75 x 12 mm timber (to make expansion joints) they can be spaced anywhere from one to three metres both for aesthetic reasons and to control shrinkage cracks). Some bitumen impregnated fibre board to fill the joints completes the requirements.

PROCEDURE

1 Compact the underlying soil using a tamper (this can be made out of a 100 x 100 mm post or pole which is used like a battering ram).

2 Lay the screeds in position, making them flush with the top of each end of the existing concrete. Check they're straight both ways. Use a string line to straighten long lengths. When correct, hold in place with well driven pegs spaced so that the screed can't deflect. Cut the pegs off level with the top of the screed. Any timber that is in contact with the concrete could be lightly oiled to lessen the chance of it sticking.

Between the screeds, tack the timber stops where the joints will be made. Make sure they are at right angles to the screed. Next cut the reinforcing mesh in position. A hacksaw will do this (although bolt cutters are faster).

3 Begin to mix the concrete (see Materials for correct mixing). Pour into position and, using the shovel to help consolidate the concrete and to remove any air bubbles, spread it making sure it is slightly full of the screeds. Lay concrete either side of the stops. Remember to lift the reinforcement.

4 When the concrete is laid, use your straight edge in a sawing action to level the concrete. Fill in all low spots. Leave it until there is no free water on the surface before you attempt to finish it with the wooden float. On cold days this may take an hour or more. Never throw neat cement on the concrete to hasten the drying or the surface will crack later.

5 If the day is hot, once the surface is finished (you may wish to go over it with a sponge to increase the surface roughness and decrease the possibility of slipping), cover it with some old plastic or a tarpaulin to delay drying and potential cracking.

If you don't have a cover, wait for three or four hours, then sprinkle it periodically with a fine spray to slow the drying process.

6 Remove the screeds and stops after 24 hours and fill the gap with the joint material. Continue to wet the concrete for several days. Don't allow foot traffic for at least 36 hours.

Break up the old concrete with a crowbar or sledge hammer.

You may have to cut through the path with an electric saw.

Compact the underlying soil with a wooden tamper.

Lay the screeds in position, using string to make them straight.

To keep the screeds in position, secure them to well driven pegs.

Lay the reinforcing mesh in position.

Mix the concrete (see Materials Section for correct mixing).

Pour the concrete into position and spread it.

Lift the reinforcing mesh after pouring the concrete.

Use your straight edge to level the concrete.

Finish the surface with a wooden float.

When set, sprinkle with a fine spray to slow the drying process.

Painting Fascias and Eaves

The outside of a house has a hard time because of sun, wind, rain and humidity and temperature extremes. Many materials, such as brick, terracotta, fibre cement and concrete, handle this with ease. Others, like timber and ungalvanised ferrous metal, don't. Certain materials therefore need to be painted periodically otherwise they quickly deteriorate.

Preparation

At the risk of being repetitious, let me make the point that the final success of the job will only be as good as the preparation. Unfortunately, if you're like me, you want to get on the end of a brush or roller and slap the paint on rather than be covered for days in dust, sandpaper grit, rust and sweat.

Proper preparation may be tedious, time-consuming, but it's essential. Unless you are a quick worker, do one side of the house at a time. This is because some primers require undercoating in less than four weeks.

Begin at the highest point (gutter) and move down to the fascia, the eaves, the windows and doors, then any feature boards or cladding. Before you begin, tie back or trim any nuisance tree, take off all flyscreens, house numbers, and cover pavers and paths with plastic sheeting, etc.

Gutters and downpipes Use a wire brush and sandpaper to remove any rust or peeling paint (after you've cleaned out the gutters). (Observe the ladder safety described in Repairing a Leaking Roof.) Treat with rust remover where necessary and then spot prime with an appropriate primer.

Fascias Burn, sand (a sanding disc in an electric drill is handy but wear a particle mask and eye goggles), wire brush or scrape off all peeling or poorly adhering paint. For paint in good condition, use sugar soap or proprietary cleaner to rid the surface of grime, then lightly sand. Spot prime any bare spots, feathering the edges off.

Windows and doors 1. Timber. Treat in the same way as fascias, but pay special attention to joints. That is where rot-inducing moisture can get in. Pay special attention to the sill. If the putty has cracked, replace it (see Glazing).

2. Steel. Use the same treatment as for gutters.

3. Aluminium. Clean with turps and fine wet-and-dry. Apply an aluminium primer.

Cladding 1. Timber. If painted, treat in the same way as fascias but remember to renail any loose boards or sheets. Then punch and fill the holes with putty. If stained, nothing more than recoating should be necessary, providing you remove wasps' nests, cocoons, etc.

2. Fibre or asbestos cement. Scrape off any loose paint and wash thoroughly with sugar soap. Lightly sand and reprime any bare patches.

With all of the above don't forget to treat areas of mould or mildew with an anti-mould preparation.

Guttering, fascia and eaves in need of a coat of paint.

Sand thoroughly to remove peeling paint and rust.

If paint is in good condition it will only need a wash.

Work from the top down. Paint guttering first.

Next paint the fascia and eaves.

Walls can be painted with a brush or roller.

PROCEDURE

The moment you've impatiently waited for has arrived! Get out the brushes, rollers, rags and tins of beautiful designer colours. Wear some old clothes and a hat.

1 The principle to be applied again is to work from the top down. Do all undercoating if necessary and make sure you use one that suits the finishing paint. Then apply finishing coats to fascias, eaves and porches, gutters, walls, windows and doors, in that order.

Regarding the paint system, can I recommend you use a water-soluble one (for starters you can clean the brushes in water). From my own experience, oil-based paints are a real pain, not only to put on, but because they tend to peel, crack and craze as the oil dries out. A weatherboard house I once owned got painted with acrylic paint once every seven years and the only preparation it required was a wash down with some detergent and a scrubbing brush. The ubiquitous 'man next door', an oil-paint advocate, had to paint his house every two years and spent several days beforehand preparing it.

2 Use paint pots rather than painting direct from the tin. Rollers are obviously far quicker than brushes for large areas and ones with long handles can make an easy job of boxed eaves. Wrap some old cloth around the top of ladders to stop marking or scratching. Brush-paint around the edges of large areas first, and then fill in the centres using the paint roller.

If the walls are too high or the job is too big, get three quotes from members of the Master Painters' Guild and be satisfied attacking something smaller — like the letterbox! If you have any problems or need more information contact the Paint Manufacturers' Association in your state or the technical section of your favourite paint company.

Laying Cork or Vinyl Tiles

Changing the colour, pattern or material used on a kitchen or family room floor can work magic. Two popular finishes are cork and vinyl.

Cork is a warm, softish, honey-coloured material but it can easily be damaged if care is not taken. Vinyl is cold, virtually indestructible and comes in an amazing range of patterns and colours.

Before making your selection of either product, bring home at least a dozen tiles. Lay them together to get some idea of the overall effect.

Tiles are typically 300 mm square and you'll need approximately 12 to the square metre. If you supply an accurate floor plan to your supplier, they will calculate both the tiles and adhesive you require.

Preparation

As with most things, the final success will depend largely on the preparation. Your existing floor will typically be made from polished boards or covered with linoleum, carpet, or vinyl asbestos tiles.

Remove the carpet (or non-glued sheet linoleum) and all staples, tacks, etc.; then check the boards for shrinkage. If the joints are relatively tight, go over the floor with rough sandpaper to clean off any irregularities and to ensure the surface is clean so that the tile glue will achieve a good bond. If there is any dampness, find the reason, correct it, then allow the patch to dry before you apply the new covering. In the case of polished floors, you should sand back to bare timber to ensure good adhesion.

Where the boards have large gaps, knot holes or cracks (or if you have old vinyl or linoleum that is well stuck down), perhaps the easiest way to obtain a good finish is to cover the entire floor with tempered hardboard or fibre cement. This will ensure that you have a smooth, clean, solid surface to stick your tiles to. Use a metal strip at doorways to finish it off neatly. If you're unlucky, you may have to take a few millimetres off the doors to stop them rubbing on the tiles.

Your tile plan will assist the hardware store or timber yard to give you hardboard sheet sizes with minimum waste.

Note. Remember to wet the sheets in accordance with the manufacturer's instructions before use (see Building Boards). Nail it down securely with cadmium-coated nails (or clouts) at, say, 150 mm centres. Make sure you stagger the sheet joints (don't put them opposite each other) otherwise the joint line may show through the tiles.

If you don't lay hardboard, then you have two options. One is to lay the new tiles over the top of the existing vinyl. This involves the difficult job of removing years of accumulated grease and wax, filling large joints, refixing loose tiles, then heavily sanding the entire surface. If the tiles have asbestos in them this could be dangerous!

Remove old floorcovering and scrape off adhesive.

Lay hardboard sheets to create a flat even surface.

Using hardboard underlay nails, nail sheets to floor.

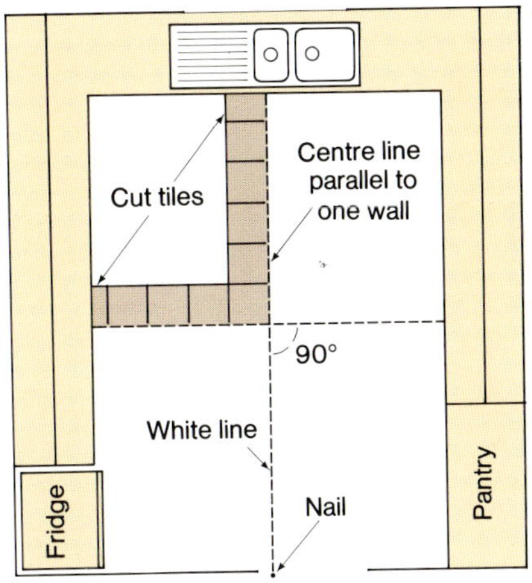

Setting out.

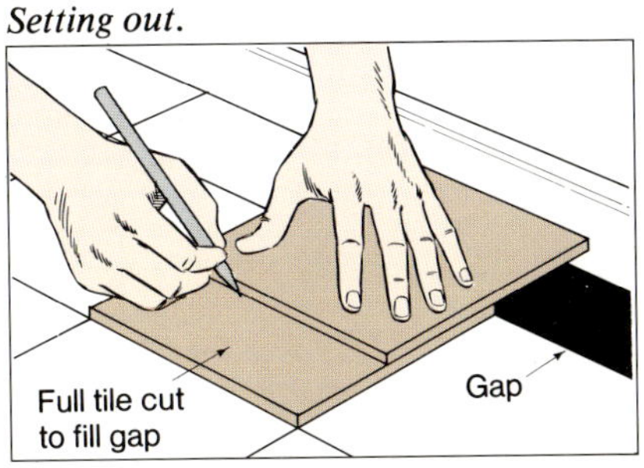

Marking tiles to complete edges.

A laundry floor brilliantly renovated with vinyl tiles.

TOOLS AND MATERIALS

A trimming knife and steel rule for cutting vinyl, panel saw for cutting cork or laying hardboard, string line and chalk, 25 mm nails, hammer, pencil and tape will be needed.

You will also need tiles and a suitable adhesive. If your supplier is doubtful about which glue to use, ring or write to the adhesive manufacturer and seek their technical advice. Sandpaper, plus nails for fixing hardboard if required, completes the requirements.

PROCEDURE

1 Pick a day when you can keep the family out of the kitchen. Look at the room dimensions and establish where the longest run of visible tiles will be. You must create a line which is in the exact centre of this area and one that runs parallel with the longest wall. This will ensure the widths of your cut tiles are roughly even and the cut edges will be against walls.

Once you have accurately established the position, drive in a nail at each end of the room, tightly stretch the chalk-filled line between them, then, pulling the line up, let it go. You should have a clear, white line on the floor.

2 Now carefully measure along this line and accurately mark its middle point. Draw another line at right angles to the white line. Here is the rule to check the lines are at right angles. From the intersection measure 3 units along one line and mark, then 4 units along the other. If the angle is a true right angle, the measurement between the marks should be equal to 5 units. For accuracy use large units. Metres would be ideal if the room is large enough. This will give you the starting position for your first tile. Lay some tiles along the white line and check how big the cut tiles will be against the walls or cupboard. If they're too small (under 50 mm), adjust to make the cut tile at one edge only.

3 Spread the glue evenly over a small area and begin to lay a row of tiles. Watch the edges stay on the white line. Alternatively you could tack down a long straight edge or batten flush with the white line and press the tiles up against this batten, and remove it once you have finished half the room.

Lay row after row of full tiles tightly together, stopping when you come to where the tiles must be cut. Then complete the other half of the room, making sure you clean off excess glue as you go.

4 To get the correct dimensions of a cut tile, lay a dry tile over a stuck one, then, using another tile pressed against wall or cupboard, draw a line. Cut along this line then apply the glue and stick the piece in position. Even intricate shapes can be marked in this way. For difficult shapes you could also make a template out of cardboard. With cork tiles, a coping saw is a useful tool to help you cut around the shape of fancy architraves.

5 Allow to dry overnight, then quickly apply the recommended finish before allowing the troops in to gasp in admiration at your cleverness and the beautiful new room!

42 825
42 854
42 837
42 860
42 847

Plugging a Hole in Timber

Often, when locks are replaced, fittings changed, or a door is removed from a jamb, there are unsightly holes left in the timber. If the hole is small — say 10 mm at its widest point — it can usually be satisfactorily plugged with putty or another appropriate filler. If it's larger than that, it is far better to fill the hole with a small block.

Neatly chisel out the waste, making sure the edges of the hole are square.

Measure, mark and cut a block to fill the hole.

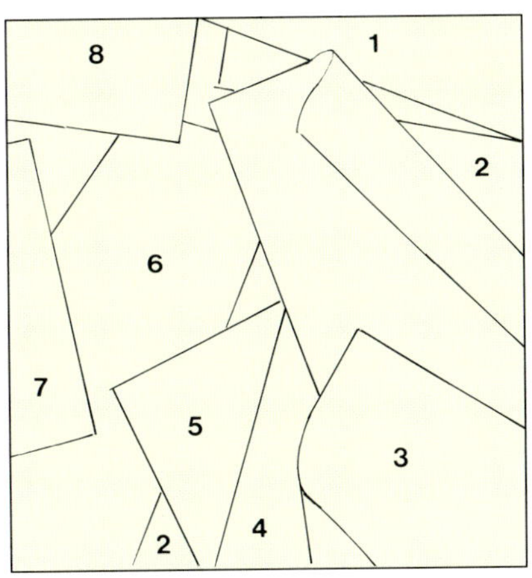

Cork and vinyl flooring
1. Raw cork floor tiles
2. Cork with polyurethane finish
3. Foam-backed vinyl
4. Marble patterned vinyl
5. Subtle Greek Key pattern
6. Inlay detail
7. Colour samples of patterned vinyl
8. Inlaid vinyl floor design

TOOLS AND MATERIALS

A sharp chisel, a plane, rule and pencil, a square, cork block and hammer are all the tools needed.

You'll need a small block of softwood which can be cut and planed to fit the hole without exposing any end grain. Use a similar species to the timber section if the wood has a clear finish. Some sandpaper and glue complete the requisites.

PROCEDURE

1 First sharpen the plane iron and chisel (see Sharpening Planes and Chisels under Hand Tools).

2 The hole must now be carefully marked out with a sharp pencil and square to make it a regular square or rectangle). It must have perfectly straight and parallel sides. Don't make it bigger than necessary!

3 With a chisel (the wider the better) and some light taps of the hammer, carefully cut around the pencil line to a depth of 0.5 mm. Make sure the bevel side of the chisel points towards the centre of the hole. Make sure you stay *inside* the lines. If one side of the hole is close to the edge, tap carefully in case you split the timber.

4 Next chisel the waste out, making sure the edges of the hole are square to the face of the timber. Take your time and don't try to take out too much at one go. Start from one end and make a deep cut. Then lay the chisel over, bevel down, and make a series of cuts working towards the other end. You'll see the timber peeling off in a series of wedges. Make sure you always keep your fingers behind the sharp edge.

Then, using both hands, push the chisel along and clean out the waste. Then, if necessary, make a slightly deeper cut.

5 When the hole is neatly cut out, measure, mark and cut the block to size, making it approximately 2 mm larger than the hole in width, thickness and length. Then plane the sides and ends down until the block fits the hole. Slightly undercut the edges so the block will, with a few taps of the hammer, wedge itself tightly into the hole.

When planing, put the block on a firm, straight surface. If you can't hold the block properly, nail a thin stop to the surface to prevent the block sliding off (see Planing Procedure in Sticking Doors).

When planing the ends, don't plane right across them or you'll split off the far edge. If you come in halfway from both sides there'll be no problems. Another way, if you have a vice, is to put a scrap piece of timber behind the edge of your block and level with it, then plane away to your heart's content.

6 Once the block is fitted, apply a generous layer of glue to the edges and ends of both the block and the hole, then tap the block into place. If it's a little loose, tack it into place with some small brads. Allow a few hours to dry.

7 To finish, plane it almost flush with the surface, then, using a cork block, sandpaper it smooth and flush. The cork block is important because it keeps the sandpaper flat and applies an even pressure which guarantees that the block will be indistinguishable from the rest of the timber section.

8 Fill any gaps with a suitable filler and then apply a finish that matches the original. If you've worked carefully the hole will have disappeared forever and you'll have gained a new and valuable skill that can be applied to recalcitrant knot holes and badly chipped edges.

APPENDIX

SAFETY IN THE HOME

A home can be sweet — but it can also injure or kill! How safe is your home for the people who live in it, the ones you really care about?

The age group most at risk is children. Children have an insatiable curiosity but little instinctive awareness of potential danger. They learn slowly so just warning them is not enough — you must protect them. Children as a risk group are closely followed by the elderly, who have learned about safety but may now be absent-minded or infirm.

Take a walk with me, room by room, and we'll check the danger potential of your home. Try to see each point from the perspective of naughty or curious children or old people who are not as alert or agile as you are. Some simple maintenance can easily reduce the risks.

The Kitchen

— Are your polished floors slippery?

— If someone slipped, are there sharp corners to fall against? Rubber edging could solve the problem.

— Do you have lockable or childproof cupboards for storing poisonous or potentially lethal cleaners, spray cans and solvents?

— Are the stools, if any, stable?

The Bathroom

— Can the hot tap on the bath be easily turned on? Do you check the bath water or shower temperature for your elderly parents? Scalding water has caused some horrendous burns.

— Can you quickly get into the bathroom from the outside if the door is accidentally locked?

— Is the bottom of your bath or shower slippery? A non-slip mat will solve the problem.

— Is your medicine cabinet childproof and kept locked at all times?

Hall and Stairs

— How good is the lighting?

— Is there a childproof gate across steep stairs?

— Is the carpet torn in such a way that tripping could occur?

Lounge and Family Room

— Are the power points childproof?

— How easy would it be for your child to get up onto the window sill?

— Could anyone run or walk through a glass door or window? Stick-on patterns make the glass more obvious. Replace the glass with safety glass if any doubt exists.

— How childproof is your drinks cabinet?

The Garage

— How many cutting tools, hand or electric, can your child get at?

— Make a list of the poisonous items that are lying about. Turps, snail pellets, weed poisons . . . it only takes one. Keep them on a high shelf or in a locked cupboard.

Well. How did you go? Were you horrified? Is your home as safe as you thought?

SAFETY REMINDERS

- Anything that is remotely dangerous for a child to eat, drink, put in their mouths or over their heads should always be kept in lockable or childproof cupboards.
- Sharp objects, tools, cutting implements or flammable substances must be made inaccessible to even the most determined and innovative child at all times.
- Floors or baths should NOT be slippery, carpets should not be wrinkled or torn, and stairs must be well-lit and blocked off to young children.
- Power points should be childproof and all leads tucked or taped out of the road.
- You should be able to turn off the main water, gas and electricity supply in a matter of seconds. Have emergency phone numbers by the phone.
- Turn all hot water taps off HARD and always supervise young children in baths and showers.
- Safety tape glass doors to make them visible.
- Windows should be able to be fixed partly open.
- You should be able to open all doors in an emergency.

There is a risk of injury with plate-glass windows if they are not marked in any way.

Fire!

The fear of death or injury from burning should motivate people to be fire conscious — yet the sound of a fire engine is commonplace in most communities.

In Australia almost 200 people die each year from fires and there are four to five times more people who become casualties, some with shocking burns. In Australia each year, around 1600 fires occur via cooking appliances and 700 are caused by heaters. Yet presenting statistics does not seem to increase caution. The attitude is that 'It will never happen to me'. As fire consumes in excess of 9000 flats and houses per year in Australia, it obviously can and does happen.

So how can you lessen the risk?

1. The kitchen stove is the major culprit. Don't overfill saucepans with flammable cooking liquids (1/3 maximum) or leave them unattended. Curtains near a stove are a no-no. Keep a fire blanket or suitable extinguisher close by.

If a fire begins, turn off the electricity or gas before trying to put a small stove fire out. Remember, NEVER USE WATER ON A FAT OR COOKING OIL FIRE. If the fire won't stop, immediately call the fire brigade. Have the number handy.

2. Heaters are next. Supervise heaters at all times especially if children are around. Keep the heater away from curtains and furniture. Open fires should have sparkproof and childproof guards. Don't carry kerosene heaters around.

3. Smoking is another major source. If you must smoke, never do it in bed, or on a flammable lounge, or over a flammable carpet.

4. Always keep matches and lighters out of the reach of children.

5. Don't do any electrical wiring unless you're qualified. Have extra power points installed rather than overload existing ones. Have all electrical and gas appliances checked regularly (including electric blankets). If the house wiring is old, get it replaced. Unplug appliances if you're going away.

6. Keep flammable substances like petrol, turps, kerosene, nail polish remover, etc., locked away. Never use petrol to start or invigorate a fire.

7. Unplug all electrical appliances if they're not being used.

8. If you live in a bushy environment, clear away all scrub and timber from near the house. Keep the grass short and free of leaves. Never store combustible materials or flammable liquids under your house. Clean gutters regularly. Use a properly constructed incinerator.

9. Have a ladder handy to reach high windows. Make sure windows allow egress. Keep a long hose permanently connected.

Smoke detectors Accidents do happen in spite of the most thorough precautions. Installation of a suitable smoke detection system can give you time to get your family out of the house. The cost is small. The average three-bedroom home requires two battery operated detectors at a cost of between $30 and $50 each. It is a small price to pay for an early warning! Your supplier will advise on the number you will need and where they should be placed.

Fire extinguishers There are a variety of extinguishers available and each one is designed to put out a particular type of fire (electric, flammable liquid, wood, etc.). Using the wrong one can actually make the fire worse! Make sure you have sufficient types of large enough capacity to fight each possible type of fire. Spread them around the home in accessible places and make sure everyone knows which ones to use. The table on the next page shows the different types and their uses in detail.

FIRE DRILL

If there's a fire, does everyone in your family know what to do? You as the responsible parent must ensure that they do. It should be regularly practised, especially with small children. This is what to do.

- Don't panic. Wake each one. Everyone should gather in a pre-arranged place on the ground floor. Do not choose the kitchen or the lounge room because most fires start there.
- When everyone is present, take them outside to safety and then call the fire brigade.
- If someone is missing, send the rest outside via a safe exit and instruct the most responsible one to call the brigade at a neighbour's. Then try to locate the missing one. If the rooms are smoky, put a wet cloth over your face. While searching, keep as close to the floor as possible. If you have time, close doors and windows behind you as you leave each room. This starves the fire of oxygen and slows the spread.

  If the fire is too hot, get out! You won't do your family any good if you become a fatality too!
- Once everyone is safe, try to investigate the cause and the extent of the fire. If it's small and you have the right extinguisher or fire blanket, attempt to put it out.
- Don't try to save possessions. Remember more than eighty per cent of deaths attributable to fire are caused not by burning but by people being overcome by smoke or toxic gas (e.g. cyanide gas comes from some cushion fillings). It only takes a few minutes!

People need fire — but it's a relationship that must be handled with extreme caution at all times.

The Correct Use of Fire Extinguishers

A fire extinguisher is an invaluable safety aid to have in the house or garage. However, it is essential to use the correct type of extinguisher for each kind of fire. The table alongside shows the different types and their applications. Check extinguishers regularly to see that they are in working order. Also make sure that everyone knows how to use them.

No attempt should be made to extinguish gas fires if the gas flow cannot be stemmed immediately.

Electrical Hazards

Extinguishers shown for C class fires in the accompanying table, and those having a letter E displayed on the extinguisher body, are suitable for use on fires involving live electrical hazards.

D CLASS FIRES

D Class involves combustible metals. Specialist advice should be sought regarding the appropriate extinguishing medium required.

BCF EXTINGUISHERS

BCF extinguishers should not be used on burning cooking oil or fat, nor on Class D fires (combustible metal). BCF is non-toxic but should be used with caution in confined spaces.

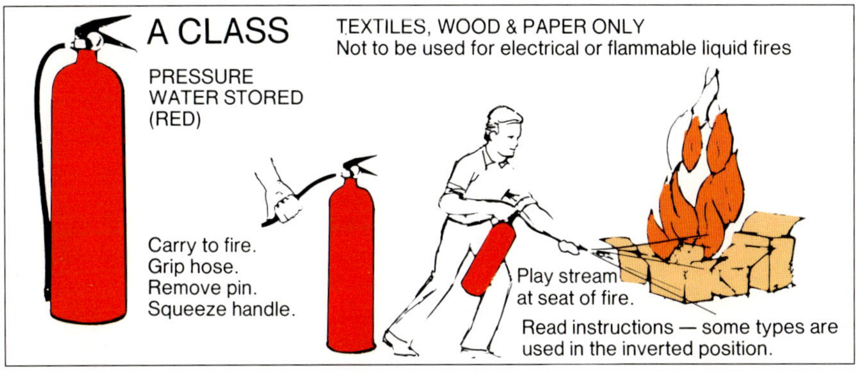

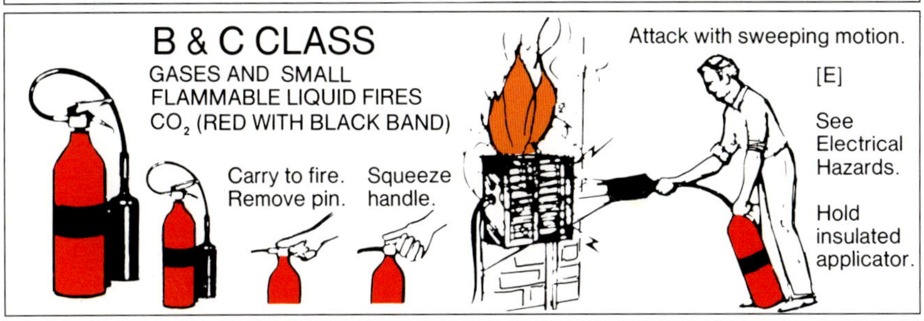

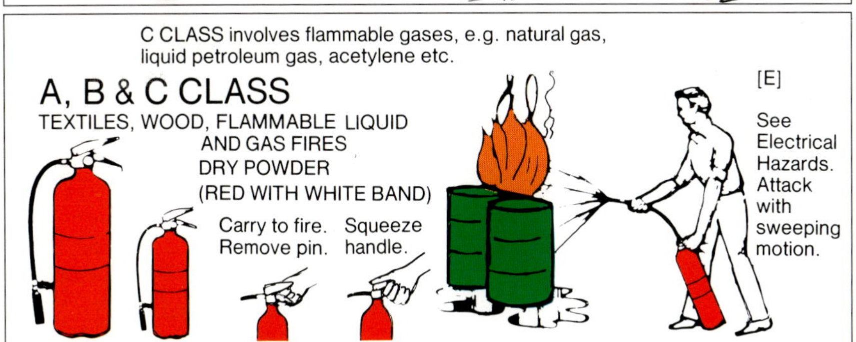

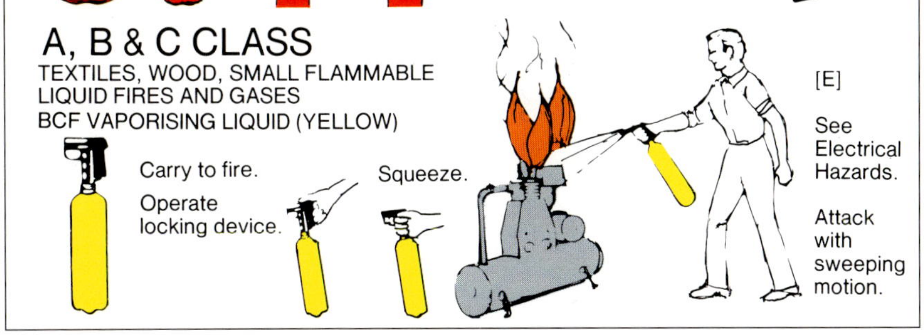

ALL EXTINGUISHERS MUST BE RECHARGED AFTER USE.

Glossary

arch bar: a flat steel bar placed under a brick flat arch to hold it in place
architrave: a moulding surrounding a doorway or window
arris: to take off a corner to provide a smooth finish

batt: a rectangular sheet of matted fibre
batten: a light strip of wood
bearer: a sub-floor timber which supports floor joists
bevel: a sloping surface; to cut at an angle of more than 90°
bolster: a wide cold chisel for cutting bricks
brad: a fine nail
brickbat: a piece of brick
butt: to place end to end

calcined: oxidised by heating
camber: a slight convexity on an upper surface
Carborundum (TM) stone: a block of silicon carbide used for sharpening tools
casement window: a side-hinged window
caulk: to fill (a joint) to make it watertight, airtight, etc.
chamfer: a small bevel or slope on a corner
chord: one of the main horizontal members of a truss
chuck: a mechanical device for holding a drill bit so that it can be rotated
cladding: the exterior covering of a wall
clenching: fastening a nail by bending the end over and beating down the point
clout: a nail with a flat round head
cold chisel: a strong chisel for cutting metal or masonry
comb chisel: a cold chisel with prongs
coping: the topmost course of masonry in a wall
cornice: a plaster moulding round a ceiling
cramp: a frame or tool which can be screwed up to hold things together; to fasten or hold with a cramp
cure: to preserve or finish by a chemical or physical process

damp proof course: a layer of moisture-proof material in a masonry wall
dovetail joint: an interlocking joint with the tenons shaped like a dove's spread tail
dowel: a round wooden pin for fastening
dowelling: long thin wooden rods
DPC: damp proof course
drip: a groove under the overhanging edge of a coping, sill, etc. to prevent water flowing back to the wall
drummy: sounding hollow, indicating a lack of bonding between layers

efflorescence: a powdery crust on the surface of masonry resulting from evaporation

fall: a downward slope
fascia: a wide board fixed to the ends of the rafters, carrying the gutter
feathering: tapering off
ferrous: containing iron
flashing: a piece of sheet metal, etc., used to make roofing joints and angles watertight
float: a wooden or metal tool for smoothing plaster or cement
flush cone: a rubber seal where the flush pipe from the cistern joins a toilet bowl
footing: the part of a wall that is in direct contact with the ground
foundation: the natural or prepared ground on which a building stands
full of: above, longer than

gain: a recess cut in timber
galvanise: to coat with metal, usually zinc
garnet paper: abrasive paper
grout: a fine finishing plaster used to fill gaps between ceramic tiles
gypsum: hydrated calcium sulphate used to make plaster

hawk: a small square board with a handle underneath, used for plaster or mortar
housed joint: a joint where the end of one board fits into a groove cut into another

ironing: making a round joint in (mortar)

jamb: the side member of a door or window frame
joist: any of the beams supporting floorboards or a ceiling

knotting: a preparation for sealing knots in timber before painting

lump hammer: a small sledgehammer

mitre: to make a right-angled joint by cutting each piece to be joined at an angle of 45°
mortice and tenon: a joint in which a tongue (the tenon) fits into a hole (the mortice)
moulding: a strip of wood for edging, finishing corners, etc., cut in various shapes

noggings: short horizontal timbers between wall studs

pier: a masonry support for floor timbers, etc.
pinch bar: a short crowbar with a U-shaped claw
plate: *see* wall plate
plugging chisel: a steel tool struck with a hammer to rake out masonry joints

quad: a moulding in the shape of a quadrant of a circle

rail: a horizontal member in a door, balustrade, fence, etc.

rake: to make a square joint in (mortar)

ratchet screwdriver: a screwdriver with a mechanism to obviate continual hand movement

rebate: a recess made to receive an edge

reveal: the vertical face of an opening for a door or window between the face of the wall and the door or window frame

riser: the vertical face of a step

scantlings: structural timbers of relatively small cross-section

scarf joint: a joint in which the ends of two pieces of wood are cut to lap over each other and then fastened together to make a continuous piece

screed: a piece of wood temporarily forming a guide for the thickness of the surface; to bring a surface to the required level

scutch: a bricklayer's cutting tool

shellac: a kind of varnish

shim: a thin piece of metal, wood, etc. used to fill in space

shiplap: boards edge-dressed to make a close-fitting rebated or lapped joint

sidings: weatherboards, etc. cladding a framed building

sprig: a small tapering headless nail

stile: an outer vertical member in a panelled door, window frame, etc.

stud: any of the main upright timbers in a wall

tongue and groove joint: a method of joining boards side by side to seal out draughts and/or hide shrinkage

tread: the part of a step that is trodden on

truss: a rigid framework of beams, struts, etc.

wall plate: a horizontal member of a wall that ties it together, distributes the pressure of joists, etc.

wet-and-dry: fine emery paper that can be used either with a lubricant to reduce clogging, or dry

ACKNOWLEDGEMENTS

The Publisher thanks the following for their help in supplying materials for the photography in this book.

Abet Laminati Print Laminate Distributors, Alexandria NSW
ACI Insulation, Dandenong Vic
Altered Image Wall Coverings & Fabrics, Artarmon NSW
Decortex Wallcoverings & Fabrics, Rosebery NSW
Johnson Tiles, Chester Hill NSW
Laminex Industries, Caringbah NSW
Makita Australia, Silverwater NSW
The Olde English Tiles Factory, Camperdown NSW
Fred Pazotti, Woollahra NSW
Pilkington (Australia), Melbourne Vic
Tarkett Australia, Chester Hill NSW
Weils Hardware, Gladesville NSW

Thanks also to the Public Relations Unit, Board of Fire Commissioners of NSW, for their assistance.

Index

Published by **Murdoch Books**, a division of Murdoch Magazines Pty Ltd
213 Miller Street, North Sydney NSW 2060

Design: Dawn Daly, Warren Penney
Commissioned Photography: Ray Joyce, Andrew Payne
Illustrations: David Stokan
Cover Design: Jan Gosewinckel
Finished Art: Dawn Daly
Index: Garry Cousins

Publisher: Anne Wilson
Production Manager: Penny Martin
Managing Editor: Maureen Colman
Marketing Manager: Mark Smith

National Library of Australia
Cataloguing-in-Publication Data
Smith, Dennis M.
Home Repairs and Maintenance
ISBN 0 86411 171 1
Includes index.
1. Dwellings — Maintenance and repair.
(Series: Australian Better Homes and Gardens
Homemaker Library.)
643.7

First published 1991
Printed by Toppan Printing Co. Ltd, Singapore
Typeset by Savage Type Pty Ltd, Brisbane

Australian distribution to supermarkets and newsagents by
Gordon & Gotch Ltd, 68 Kingsgrove Road, Belmore NSW 2192

* Recommended and maximum price only.